The Brass Tacks Guide to Writing a Winning Business Plan

TODD HOUSTON SMITH

Brass Tacks Books

Names: Smith, Todd Houston, author.
Title: The brass tacks guide to writing a winning business plan / Todd
Houston Smith.
Description: Jacksonville, FL : Brass Tacks Books, 2021.
Identifiers: ISBN 978-1-7353059-3-6 (paperback) | ISBN 978-1-7353059-5-0
(ebook)
Library of Congress Control Number: 2021909987
Subjects: LCSH: Business planning. | Small business. | Entrepreneurship.
| Venture capital. |
    Marketing. | BISAC: BUSINESS & ECONOMICS / Strategic
Planning. | BUSINESS &
    ECONOMICS / Small Business. | BUSINESS & ECONOMICS /
Entrepreneurship. |
    BUSINESS & ECONOMICS / Marketing / General.
Classification: LCC HD30.28 .S65 2021 (print) | LCC HD30.28 (ebook) |
DDC 658.4/012--dc23.

Brass Tacks Books
1100 Shetter Ave, Suite #205
Jacksonville Beach, FL 32250

brass tacks plural noun

 Save Word

Definition of *brass tacks*

: details of immediate practical importance —usually used in the phrase *get down to brass tacks*

ABOUT BRASS TACKS BOOKS

Our goal at Brass Tacks Books is to provide you with books about the worlds of entrepreneurship, business, direct investing, and wealth creation. Not only that, we want to give you information in an unfiltered way - raw, succinct, direct, and actionable. Time is precious, and we don't want to fill the pages of our books with fluff or filler just to make it look like you're getting more. There will be stories to emphasize particular points and to make them more real, and this is part of any real-world learning.

Our goal is to help you succeed, to put you on a path to success, financial freedom, abundance, and prosperity. With the rare exceptions of strokes of good luck, obtaining these things generally involves an ugly four-letter word: work. If you're looking for someone to blow smoke and sunshine up your tailpipe, or fill you full of false dreams of fancy cars, yachts, and lifestyles of the rich and arrogant, or for someone to give you a magic easy button, you've come to the wrong place.

That's not to say that achieving one's dreams has to involve decades of toil and grind, either. Working smart is highly preferable to working hard. And making the most valuable use of one's most limited resource, time, is the primary objective.

That said, we believe that entrepreneurship and the activities that stem from it are one of the world's most prominent driving forces for good. Free markets and the free enterprise system, under proper governance, inspire innovation, create jobs, spur new technologies and make the world a better place for all.

The global economy is not a zero-sum game, where there are only winners and losers and only a limited pie to be fought and wrestled over. Instead, it is one of ever-increasing abundance, where everyone can benefit and have better lives, if we take care of each other and of the planet on which we live.

When you invest in real estate, you put tradespeople to work, you feed the economy, you provide comfortable places for people to live, work, recreate, and shop. You improve neighborhoods, cities, states, and countries.

When you start and grow a business or invest in one, you create jobs, support families, and you foster creativity, innovation, and technology. In short, you make the world a better place. In the process, you create a better life for yourself and your family, and once you gain true financial freedom, perhaps you can put your excess resources to good use to extend your legacy.

Who Am I and Why You Should Listen to Me

You may be wondering who I am and why I am writing this book. I'll tell you more about me at the end of the book, but very briefly, I am a licensed Florida real estate broker and owner of Blue Horizon Real Estate. I also founded Blue Horizon Property Solutions, a real estate investment company. These companies have closed hundreds of millions of dollars of transactions in three states, both commercial and residential, including historical property. My specialty is investment real estate.

I am also the CEO of Blue Horizon Venture Consulting, where I work with early-stage companies. I have more than 20 years of experience working with high-growth firms, and my work has helped entrepreneurs start or grow hundreds of businesses in 33 US states and 16 countries around the world. These firms have helped to raise hundreds of millions in capital and have employed thousands of people. I am also the author of **The Adventure Consultant, The Brass Tacks Guide to Real Estate Entrepreneurship** and the host of the **Brass Tacks Business** podcast.

My aim is to help you succeed, no matter what your chosen occupation. Now let's get down to details of immediate practical importance: The Brass Tacks of a Writing a Winning Business Plan.

brass tacks plural noun

 Save Word

Definition of *brass tacks*

: details of immediate practical importance —usually used in the phrase *get down to brass tacks*

FOREWORD

WHY BUSINESS PLANS ARE, AND ALWAYS WILL BE, NECESSARY AND WHY EVERY BUSINESS SHOULD HAVE ONE.

Disclaimer: I write business plans for a living and have been doing it for over two decades. My plans have helped build factories in Chile, roll out high speed internet in Armenia, turn a crumbling 500-yr-old Hacienda in Mexico into a 5-star resort, build townhomes in Romania, and they have helped hundreds of businesses across almost every state in the U.S. and many other countries around the world. My clients have raised hundreds of millions of dollars and have created thousands of jobs.

So, do I have skin in this game? Sure I do, let's be real. But please hear me out, because this topic goes way beyond my business to one of the fundamental factors of business success.

Of the strategic and funding packages we build, around 55% of our clients succeed with their strategic objective, be it raising outside capital, or creating organic internal growth. To put that in perspective, less than ½ one 1% of all business plans written ever achieve their objectives. So our success rate is about 100x better than average.

In order to offset any perception of potential bias, let's look at some statistics about business plans:

> Companies that created plans were twice as likely to grow their business or obtain capital as those that didn't.

Palo Alto Software found that companies that created plans were twice as likely to grow their business or obtain capital as those that didn't. Right off the bat, you have DOUBLE the chance of success.

In a study from the *Journal of Business Venturing*, more than 11,000 companies were surveyed, and the study showed than business planning has a clear impact on business performance. Interestingly, it showed an even greater impact for existing businesses than it did for startups.

Another study from the *Journal of Management Studies* concluded that business planning helped companies grow 30% faster than companies who had no plan. To put that in perspective, let's say two startups hit first year revenue targets of $1 million. Startup A grew for the next four years at 20%, while startup B, with a business plan in place, grew at a 26% clip. At the end of the 5th year, startup A saw revenues of $2.07 million. Startup B realized $2.52 million in revenues. Let's further assume that both founders want to exit their businesses at the end of year five and that the going rate in their industry is 8X top line revenues. Startup A's founder walks away with a cool $16.6 million. Not bad. Startup B's founder, however, pockets more than $20.2 million, a factor of accelerated growth that was born from smart business planning. I don't know about you, but I wouldn't mind having almost $4 million more to start my next venture or to do some good in the world!

An article from *Harvard Business Review* talks about the Panel Study of Entrepreneurial Dynamics where they sampled 1,000 new entrepreneurs over a six-year period, one of the most comprehensive studies ever done. Startup entrepreneurs who wrote formal business plans were 16% more likely to reach cash flow positivity than entrepreneurs who did not.

Run those numbers up against those of the Bureau of Labor Statistics. 20% of new businesses fail in their first year. 50% fail within 5 years. There are more than 30 million businesses in the United States alone and many more around the world. That failure rate means thousands fail EVERY DAY. Many don't have to.

Here's the problem. It takes a pretty significant skill set to write a compelling business plan.

1) Writing
2) Financial Modeling (right brain versus left brain)
3) Market Research
4) Analysis (to synthesize market research)
5) Operations
6) Marketing
7) Investor Relations
8) Law
9) Economics
10) Product Development
11) Real Estate

While you may be lucky enough to possess the skill sets to do all this work (pat yourself on back), the alternative is to work with someone who does, or to hire people onto your team who can help you and make it a team exercise.

Let's shift gears and talk specifically about startups.

In the early 2000's the methodology of lean startups came along, and with it, the false notion that business plans were no longer necessary, that investors no longer wanted to see them, and that you could magically make all your dreams come true with a handful of slides in a PowerPoint pitch deck.

It may be true that investors no longer wanted to read business plans. This is in large part because the vast majority of them are so poorly written. It was a laborious and painful exercise for them to plow through volumes of pages of fluff and hype. OK, fine, makes sense. Investors simply want to know the essence of your idea, to see if it makes sense for them to pursue any further. They have a need to filter so that they can spend the bulk of their time on the businesses of interest to them.

But what happens if you get their interest?

They are going to probe further. They are going to want more information, they want to know that you know your market, your customers, your competition, your numbers, your operating plan, your marketing plan, etc, etc.

But let's take a few steps back and talk about how early-stage ventures get funded these days and how the Lean Startup and MVP (Minimum Viable Product) concepts fit into that.

The Funding Ladder

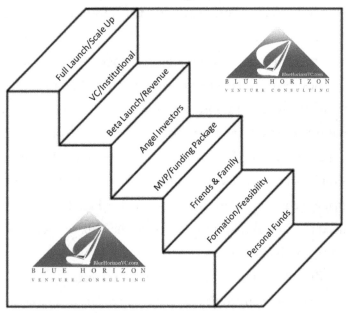

This is what I call the "Funding Ladder," and most of the entrepreneurs I see fall on their faces, usually do so, because they somehow think they can skip steps and just take ideas or concepts to venture capitalists for funding, and that they will just pull out checkbooks and write huge checks. Unless you are a one in a million entrepreneur with a long track record of successful exits, that's not going to happen.

There is a logical progression here and many people I see fail because they insist on trying to skip steps - looking to raise capital from Angels and VCs on a concept, not putting their own skin in the game, or thinking they can raise any kind of serious money on a pitch deck, without having done any of the work to back it up. Of course, they could also have a crappy idea, or one that is not generally scalable or appealing to investors as well.

So, you need to start with a feasibility study - to understand your industry, market, customers and competition. This leads you to a go-no go decision. At that point, you can research your customer base to find out what they want and work to build an MVP. As you do that work, you also need to be building your business plan, the financial and strategic backbone of your business. The ideal is to beta test your MVP, get some early customers on board and show that your product or service has some sort of market acceptance. At that point, you're ready for the next stage of raising serious capital to achieve rapid growth and scale. But along the way, you either have to self-fund your early growth, or you need to be able to attract capital from friends, family, and your intimate networks.

Now let's talk about an existing business.

Most existing business owners don't have business plans. They're too busy handling the day-to-day functions of their companies, too caught up in minutia, and many of them don't spend nearly enough of their time developing their business. Instead, they are simply operating their business. Herein lies the distinction between a business owner and an entrepreneur.

Business owners have essentially created jobs for themselves. Is that a step up from working for "the man"? Sure. But a modest one that sometimes comes with a lot more added stress and pressure.

> True entrepreneurs look ahead. They envision growth, new challenges, new ideas, better ways of doing things, incorporating new technologies, reaching new customers.

True entrepreneurs look ahead. They envision growth, new challenges, new ideas, better ways of doing things, incorporating new technologies, reaching new customers. Their companies can exist and operate without them. And, they plan.

The sad truth is that most business plans are done at startup, then they sit on a shelf gathering dust, never to be heard from again.

I should take a moment to distinguish between a capital raising business plan and an operating business plan for a going concern. The audiences are different, as is the level of detail. That's not to say that a capital raising plan can't easily be expanded into an operating plan.

Either way, these are living, breathing documents, meant to serve as frameworks for success, meant to be updated, meant to be reviewed, meant to be benchmarked against what actually happens. And there's tremendous value in planning, be it with the intent of raising capital or for strategic growth. The statistics don't lie.

Reality happens, things change, pivots become necessary, especially in a world of black swan events, and converging technologies.

There will always be contrarians out there, and their goal is to gain attention by being contradictory or controversial. It sells their books. If your goal is to succeed, to build a sustainable business, to reach cash flow positivity, and to build value in your company, planning will always be your friend. Provided you execute on those plans.

CONTENTS

1

INTRODUCTION

My first entrepreneurial experience was in 1979. I grew up in the town of York, Pennsylvania in a quiet neighborhood near York Hospital and York College. Instability in Iran had caused a huge increase in oil prices that year, and in Pennsylvania, this led to gasoline rationing and odd-even sales, where you could only purchase gas on certain days, depending on whether the numbers on your car's license plate were odd or even.

At the bottom of our hilly neighborhood was a Gulf gas station, and during this crisis, cars would line up out the gas station parking lot, around the corner, and up the hill in our neighborhood, often a long way up the hill. Occasionally, there would be 20, 30, even 40 cars in line in the neighborhood. Cars back then guzzled a lot of gas, so perhaps the hill saved all the people idling in line from having to run their engines. They could just coast down the hill.

As a 9-year-old, this was quite the phenomenon. All these people from all over town, in OUR quiet neighborhood! We'd never seen so much action! After a day or two of watching this, suddenly, inspiration struck. All these people sitting in their cars for an hour or more, they must be thirsty! Maybe even hungry!

With this in mind, I teamed up with a girl on our block who was a little older, our parents staked us some money to buy supplies, and I borrowed my Dad's well-worn red wheelbarrow. Across the street from the Gulf station was a Super Thrift grocery store, where we stocked up on coffee, lemonade, and doughnuts, after furious debate on what these drivers might want.

The next morning, we stirred up a batch of lemonade, got one of our moms to fill a thermos full of hot coffee, and we loaded it all into the wheelbarrow with the doughnuts, napkins, and cups with a handmade sign - $0.25 each! As it happened, pretty much no one could turn down two cute kids serving them car side, with something most of them wanted anyway.

Turns out, we had grossly underestimated the demand, and we sold out in perhaps 20 minutes, not even completing a full pass of the entire line. We had raked in about $25 in almost no time, even charging a quarter each for a doughnut or a drink. Most people ordered multiple things. Some even told us to keep the change!

To kids in the 70's, $25 was an unfathomable fortune. We paid back our parents, used the remaining proceeds to go back to the store, and the next day, we were back in action. We made even more! But we were not doing this in a vacuum and our little monopoly lasted only a few days. Other kids started to take notice. They, too, could go to the store, mark up the cost, and do what we were doing. Soon, we had competition.

That, too, was short-lived, as gas rationing didn't last too long, and soon the long lines and backups into the neighborhood were gone. I think we even ended up getting stuck with a fair amount of inventory, that our families ended up consuming over time.

It was a fabulous and exciting learning experience, and it was also instructive in that we really had no plan. We just ran our little enterprise by the seat of our pants, and quickly found out what happened when you miscalculated demand, failed to pay attention to competitors, or know where your customers are going to come from long term. Just as quickly as the lines of cars appeared in our neighborhood, they were gone, and so was our business.

The moral of the story is - always have a plan.

■ ■ ■

Hi. And welcome to the Brass Tacks Guide to Writing a Winning Business Plan!

This book is meant to serve as a guide for creating your own investor ready, winning strategic business plan. What are some of the things we're going to learn?

First of all, you're going to learn how to create a very extensive, detailed Excel financial model that has taken us many years to develop. In fact, if you visit our website, www.BrassTacksBooks.com/WWBP, you can even acquire the base model we work from, so that you can build yours as we go! Or, feel free to create your own.

Preparing a five-year financial forecast allows you to do some critical thinking about your business and sets the table for the rest of the plan.

We're going to teach you how to do research so that you understand the current market, what's happened in the past, and what's forecast to happen in the future.

We will research avatar customers and the competitive landscape of your business.

Then, we'll dive into the business plan template itself, which you can also obtain from the website www.BrassTacksBooks.com/WWBP.

We'll go through an operating plan, a marketing plan, and a management team.

Then, we'll discuss all the risks and mitigating factors that might affect your business.

Finally, we'll circle back to build your hard hitting, two-page executive summary.

Once your plan is complete, we will look at various graphics and editing to really dress up your plan and give it a lot of visual appeal.

The result of all this work is going to be a world-class business plan package.

Think of this as a step-by-step guide.

When possible, we'll share pictures and graphics to assist you on your journey. We'll also recommend some excellent free and paid websites you can use to help the cause.

The focus of this book is to help you reach your goals and dreams through your business. By the end of this book, you'll know how to create a great plan that gives you the best chance of raising capital. It also gives you a strategic road map that you can follow throughout the life of your business.

All this said, many people still need help, and that's entirely understandable. Our sister company, Blue Horizon Venture Consulting, is here for you if you get stuck. Please visit us at www.BlueHorizonVC.com or give us a call at 904-372-9222. We offer online courses, group consulting, and done for you individualized consulting to get you on your way. See the last chapter for more details on how we can help!

Before we get started, a word of caution. I once purchased a four-unit commercial building in New Orleans that had long been neglected. I was going to fix it up and turn it into a strong cash-flowing property. But there was so much work needed! Four bathrooms, four kitchens, restoration of oak flooring, painting inside and out, and a thousand little odds and ends. Taken as a whole, the project was sort of overwhelming.

> Building a good business plan is no different. Focus on one section at a time, bring your energy to each, and knock them out one by one.

Broken into bite-sized pieces with an action plan and schedule, I managed to start knocking things out and eventually got the project completed. Building a good business plan is no different. Focus on one section at a time, bring your energy to each, and knock them out one by one. Pretty soon, you'll have a completed work that will impress investors, stakeholders, and your operating team. Try to gloss over things just to get it done, and you'll wind up with an unappealing, half-finished work.

2

THE INITIAL FINANCIAL MODEL

Financial Assumptions

The assumptions that you make about your business are really what drives the financial model and essentially forms the skeleton or backbone of your entire business plan.

That's why it's essential to do this first before you do anything else with a business plan.

When we're working with a client, we sit the client down or get on a phone call and we spend 60 to 90 minutes going through every single detail of the expectations they have for their business.

What are they going to sell?

How much are they going to charge for it?

How many units of that product or service are they going to sell over the first five years of the business?

We try to flesh out every assumption that we can, starting with revenue assumptions, expenses, capital expenditures, human resource costs - the number of employees you're going to have and what you're going to pay them.

Herein lies a critical point with a financial model. Many people make the mistake of planning very short term: what they're going to do next month, the next quarter, or maybe the next year. Let's put that to rest right here. You need to think forward for at least five years, and you need to think big about what you want your business to become.

> You need to think forward for at least five years, and you need to think big about what you want your business to become.

This is beyond critical for the success of your venture. People who can't get out of the short-term mindset, will end up with short term results, and often, failure. Don't just think about who you need to hire to get your business started. Think about who you'll need to hire to take your business to the next level, then the next level beyond that.

You want to think big, but you also want to have reasonable and justifiable assumptions, or investors will jump all over you, and you will walk away empty-handed.

Once we put all this information together, we now have a solid financial model, from which we can learn a lot. We gain an understanding of the value of the business (good for negotiations, and the fatal flaw of most entrepreneurs who appear on *Shark Tank*). We learn how much cash we're going to need, and when, in order to keep our heads above water. We can perform simulation analysis to see what happens when we increase/decrease prices, pump up or cut sales, or hire a lot of people or very few. This knowledge is priceless, and therein lies the value of doing this work.

Over the years, we've found that going through this process is extremely helpful for clients, because it forces the client to do a lot of critical thinking about their business.

In most cases, it is thinking they haven't done before, and it forces them to envision what their business is going to look like down the road. That's why we start the process with this work - because of that critical thinking.

It's much easier to do that thinking first than halfway through the plan and realize that that you've been focused in all the wrong areas, and the plan is not heading in the direction you want.

Another point to make here is that your financial model is not set in stone, but it is constantly evolving as you go through this process. The idea is that you come back to the model as you gather more intelligence information and as you do research on your market, customers, & competition.

At the very end of the process, you come back and fine tune all those assumptions one more time.

When your assumptions are backed up by market data, then you'll bring the plan, the assumptions, and the financials into sharper focus, and you'll also be able to defend the financial assumptions that you make.

Revenue Assumptions

Perhaps one of the most enjoyable exercises is creating the revenue assumptions. This answers the essential question of how you will make money.

You want to think of every conceivable stream of revenue that generates cash for your business over the course of the next five years. Again, this is not just on the day you open your doors for business, but streams that may not start for a few years down the road.

You want to incorporate this into your financial model. You may have one or two core products or services starting in year one, and then you may add another in year two, and another in year three and build from that. Or, you may be opening a restaurant, and two years after getting things up and going, you decide to open a few more locations. Or, you decide to launch a franchise.

Remember, you're always looking forward for five years. In general, that's a realistic time horizon for You're business plan. So, if you're a startup, it's how things will grow for the first five years, and if you're an existing business, it reflects how you're going to expand from your current state.

> If you're selling the same amount at the same prices in year five as you are in year one, you haven't created a business, you've created a job, and chances are pretty good your boss is incompetent.

For each stream of revenue, you want to develop price and volume assumptions over the course of five years, and as a rule, most prices rise as do sales volumes, over time. If you're selling the same amount at the same prices in year five as you are in year one, you haven't created a business, you've created a job, and chances are pretty good your boss is incompetent.

There may be, of course, other variables that make your financial model more complicated. But for our purposes, we're going to keep things simple. If you have a complex model that requires additional help, feel free to check out the additional tools and resources at www.BrassTacksBooks.com/WWBP or you can visit our sister consulting company www.BlueHorizonVC.com and we'll be happy to chat with you and give you a few pointers - on the house!

Expense Assumptions

Whereas revenue models tend to be straightforward, expenses can be a lot more complicated. You have a lot of different categories that you need to think about:

- Cost of Goods Sold (COGS) - This is kind of the primary cost of delivering your goods or service. Think about a manufacturing business. COGS would include the cost of raw materials. It would include other processes that you have to undergo. Actual COGS numbers are preferable, but often we must estimate these as a percentage of revenues. For instance, you might estimate that web hosting and IT are going to cost you 10% of your revenues. It's always worth considering that at some point, a potential investor is going to ask you how you arrived at a particular number. You had better be prepared with an answer.

- Human Resources - This is usually a major expense for most companies. All the people you're going to need to hire over the first five years of your business, how much you expect to pay them, and when you expect to hire them. There are also taxes and benefits associated with hiring employees. Traditionally a plug of 18% works to cover this, when added on top of salary. Your situation may differ and perhaps you want to offer more benefits to attract employees.

- Recurring operating expenses - These are things such as travel, office supplies, cell phones, land-lines, website hosting, utilities, insurance, mainte-nance, etc.

- Marketing expenses - This is a big one. And again, you may want to start by plugging in some num-bers on the front end, and then once you dig into the marketing section of your plan and develop a more robust marketing plan, you'll want to come back and revise those numbers. Categories include online advertising, traditional forms of advertis-ing, postage, website development, trade show dis-plays and any other programs you're going to use to drive business.

- Real Estate/Rent - This can be a large factor, whether you're renting office space or if you are buying a building. In some businesses, real estate can be a substantial part of the business value. Debt service, down payment, and corporate income taxes are all impacted. Here the type of entity you use may also affect you. If it's a pass-through entity, you might get some tax benefits of ownership that you might not get in a C-Corporation that owns real estate.

- Taxes - Taxes play a big part of the net profitability of a business. Early-stage losses can be used to offset income later in the lifecycle of the business. Likewise, planning your major purchases around year end, can help offset the tax expense for that tax year. Again, a pass-through entity versus a stand-alone C-Corp also matters. Where you are located and whether there is a state or local tax can also have an impact. Years ago, a general plug number of 30% of income was used to cover a company's entire tax burden, but recent tax cuts have lowered that number to closer to 20%. This, of course, can be subject to change based on the whims of politics, so it is a good idea to check before you model.

- Outsourcing - The digital age has brought about a huge shift to outsourced services, which can often be cheaper than hiring employees, less fraught with risk, while allowing for the elimination of payroll taxes and benefits. Legal, accounting, marketing, PR, IT, and other functions are frequently outsourced. Make sure that you account for these costs.

- Miscellaneous - Having a plug number for the miscellaneous expenses that invariably arise in business is a good idea, whether as a percentage or periodic cost. If you don't incur them, great, but if you do, it won't break your model.

It is always best to err on the side of caution and be conservative, as it gives investors who look at your plan a sense that you're being realistic. But you don't want to be so overly conservative that you hurt your valuation. Investors are going to try to discount your forecast regardless of what you do, but if you can readily defend your assumptions, you put yourself in a much better negotiating position. Seasoned investors can tell when founders overestimate their numbers to make their model look better. They can see right through that, and you will likely lose all credibility if you do it, or if you can't defend your assumptions. Worse yet, is just plugging in "pie in the sky" numbers without any rationalization.

The Financial Model - Assumptions Page

One of the most frequent mistakes entrepreneurs make with their financials is they fail to show their core assumptions in one place. Maybe their logic was perfectly sound, but if investors must search for it or try to reverse engineer it, it's a problem.

Consider this example. A few years ago, I was thinking about starting a business called NeurTours. Who knows, by the time you read this, maybe I've already launched it. It's a way for entrepreneurs to get together, go on an adventure travel trip, unplug completely from ever-present technology, and just laser focus on how to improve their businesses, while in the process of doing something really cool. Perhaps climbing Mount Kilimanjaro, paddling a raft down the Mississippi River, or a long cycling tour.

We're going to come up with some cool adventures, and if you're not familiar with masterminding, I definitely suggest you check it out, whether you're a startup, or you've been in business for 30 years. It's amazing what happens when you get collective brain power into one room or, in the case of NeurTours, into one boat or onto one mountain. And you spend some time intermittently kind of talking about business and sharing ideas. We'll use this example throughout the book just so you can get a sense of a real-world application when building your plan.

So back to the assumptions - with NeurTours, we'll derive income from weeklong mastermind trips - run several times a year, and three-day long weekend trips for the seriously time challenged who just can't break away for an entire week. Perhaps we'll drive some ancillary revenues from things like a membership program, merchandise, and perhaps some VIP treatments like luggage and equipment services, transfers, etc. Then, perhaps we'll purchase a travel agency, and have all participants' travel flow through us with travel commissions accruing to the company. Planning all the ways you can drive revenues profitably will help you get the most out of your business.

> Planning all the ways you can drive revenues profitably will help you get the most out of your business.

I estimate the price of a weeklong trip to be $10,000. And I'll bump that up 5% per year, kind of accounting for inflation and cost of fuel. As with any business, price should be driven on perceived customer value, not some sort of cost-plus formula, but that's a topic that could likely fill an entirely different book. The three-day mastermind weekends will cost roughly $5,000. Memberships will be $50/mo., or $500/year if paid in advance, and in addition to a newsletter, members get first crack at new adventures plus perhaps a single 10% discount off a trip for each 12 months of paid membership. Merchandise, perhaps $200/year per member, and $100/year per non-member. With the travel agency, figure average cost per tour in commission-able travel is $2000 at a 5% commission per participant.

There could be some additional revenue streams in there from joint ventures, affiliates and other sources, but we'll keep it simple for the purposes here.

We're assuming that we're going to have 10 attendees per trip. In the first year, there will be three trips. Five trips in second year, then 6, 8, and 10 in years three four and five. For three-day weekends we'll run three trips in the first year and ramp up to 16 by year five. We're assuming that most of the people attending will join the membership so they can come back for future trips or stay apprised of what's going on and just be part of an exclusive club. So, here's a summary of how that looks in the model:

Revenue Model	2025	2026	2027	2028	2029	Comments
Sales Volume						
7-Day Masterminds	30	50	60	80	100	Assume 10 Per Trip
3-Day Mastermind Weekends	30	60	80	120	160	Assume 10 Per Trip
Memberships	25	50	100	150	200	
Merchandise	100	200	300	400	500	
Price Structure						
7-Day Masterminds	$10,000	$10,500	$11,025	$11,576	$12,155	5% Annual Price Increase
3-Day Mastermind Weekends	$5,000	$5,250	$5,513	$5,788	$6,078	5% Annual Price Increase
Memberships	$500	$525	$551	$579	$608	5% Annual Price Increase
Merchandise	$150	$158	$165	$174	$182	5% Annual Price Increase

As for expenses, the main expense will be trip costs, which are basically the cost for lodging, the cost of food, transportation that we provide, and anything we must pay the outfitters or to the expedition companies.

We're assuming that there's going to be a decrease as we kind of ramp up in volume, that we're going to have a little more buying power. We're eventually going to be able to negotiate better deals with the travel providers.

COGS	2025	2026	2027	2028	2029
Trip Expenses					
Costs for Trips (% of Revenue)	50.00%	48.00%	46.00%	43.00%	40.00%

The next big section is operating expenses, and employee-related operating expenses in particular. This is where you want to figure how many people you're going to hire over the first five years.

As with many startups, I plan to go it alone in the first year. I'll run all three trips and I'm not going to have any assistance. Running a mastermind group requires some skill, and doing it within the context of a trip with complex logistics, perhaps even more so.

As I go forward in the second year, I'll look to bring on an executive assistant. To be quite honest, I would probably hire that person sooner rather than later, knowing how difficult logistics can be. Having someone to take calls, book reservations, and put out the inevitable fires that arise is invaluable.

Eventually, I'll need other leaders/mastermind facilitators. It's possible some may even come from the ranks of the original trip participants. So, I'll need to hire people who are skilled in both adventure travel and also in facilitating masterminds.

These people are going to be salaried as well, and they're going to be running these trips for me so that I can kind of scale back my involvement to some extent. By the third or fourth year, I may not be running any trips.

We'll also bring on trip assistants in the second year. Here again, I may decide I need help sooner rather than later. These are people that can kind of assist with the logistics and the food and everything else and kind of make it a really smooth process and fun for everybody. Will look for really fun, energetic, and bubbly personalities as that is not my particular strong suit.

Once you've thought through your staffing needs, then it's time to think about salaries. I'm not expecting to pay myself a lot from this. I'm going to own the business. As a business owner, salary gets taxed pretty heavily, whereas dividend distributions and capital gains get taxed less. The IRS tends to frown if you take no salaried compensation, but there's a fair balance in there somewhere.

The facilitators will either have to be trained up, or they will come in with some of those skills. They also will need to handle themselves on the road, perhaps be CPR certified, and must be able to think on their feet. The trip assistants won't be paid a ton. They're getting a cool free trip out of the deal and some invaluable experience. Perhaps college age kids, or seasonal travel workers would be a good fit. Anyone who's adventurous and good working with people.

In addition, you have to think about benefits and payroll taxes. Benefits might include vacation, health care, etc. Given this won't likely be a full-time gig for anyone, perhaps the benefit load won't be too high, but you still must pay payroll tax, unless you can get away with paying people as contractors. Here that may well be possible if they are compensated on a trip-by-trip basis. Most businesses probably can't get away with that. So, in this case, I would set my benefits and payroll burden number at 15%. Most businesses are probably closer to 20%.

Employee-Related Operating Expense:	2025	2026	2027	2028	2029
Year-End Headcount					
General & Admin	2025	2026	2027	2028	2029
President	1	1	1	1	1
Executive Assistant	-	1	1	1	1
Crew					
MM Facilitators	-	1	2	2	3
Trip Assistants	-	1	2	2	3
Total Year End Headcount.............................	1	4	6	6	8
Average Base Salary by Position					
General & Admin	2025	2026	2027	2028	2029
President & Captain	40,000	46,000	52,900	60,835	69,960
Executive Assistant	30,000	34,500	39,675	45,626	52,470
Crew					
MM Facilitators	50,000	57,500	66,125	76,044	87,450
Trip Assistants	20,000	23,000	26,450	30,418	34,980
Benefits & Payroll Taxes	15%				

General and administrative expenses fall into a number of categories. Supplies, travel, phone, postage, utilities, maintenance/repairs, insurance, training/development, and the all-important "Miscellaneous" category. Remember, this is a business forecast, so don't get caught up too much in the weeds of infinite detail. You don't have to call your ISP and find out to the penny how much your internet service is going to cost. Just account for it along with other utilities. In our model, we base these expenses on the number of employees in the company. You can also estimate exact amounts, although these types of expenses do tend to be variable, and headcount is usually a good determinant of these costs.

Capital purchases should be considered separately. We likely will have to go out and buy some equipment for the business. Perhaps a van, perhaps a boat, maybe a trailer for bikes/kayaks. Then there are office equipment costs for computers and other hardware, software, and furniture. All these things are assets on your balance sheet and are depreciable, which helps offset some taxes.

Next you need to think about your marketing expenses. Here we have print advertising, direct mail, online pay per click, website development, brochures, events/trade shows, etc. Developing a comprehensive marketing plan and sales operation is important to keeping your pipeline full of customers. If you don't have such a plan, then you tend to lurch from customer to customer, often with lulls in between.

Capital Purchases

Equipment Purchases per New Employee	Hardware	Software	Furniture & Fixtures
General & Admin	300	300	300
Boat & One Time Costs	$10,000		

Depreciation	
Hardware	3 years
Software	3 years
Furniture & Fixtures	7 years

Marketing Expenses

Advertising Expenses	Per Month	Beginning	Annual Increase
Print Advertising	3,000	Jan-25	10%
Direct Mail Advertising	1,000	Feb-25	10%
Online Advertising (PPC, etc.)	1,000	Mar-25	15%
One-time Expenses (Web Site, Brouchures, etc)	$5,000		
Annual Expenditures (Local Events)	$5,000		

Insurance and real estate are also big considerations for many businesses. Whether you rent an office or buy one (which can be a profitable venture of its own), you'll need to factor this in, unless you plan to operate out of your home. Even then, there are some tax advantages to utilizing part of your home for a business, but it's a tricky topic, so best to consult with a CPA. Insurance is also a big item. With NeurTours, liability is certainly a concern and must be covered. Having the proper legal contracts with participants is also important to protect the business in the off chance that something unfortunate happens during one of the trips. If you do enough of them, eventually something is going to happen that you didn't anticipate.

If you are using any sort of financing, you'll want to account for those costs in your model. Likewise, if you carry any sort of cash balance, you'll want to try to earn some sort of return on that capital versus having it sitting idle. You'll also need to forecast your tax burden, local, state, and federal. Here you can plug a percentage of net operating income, usually in the 20-30% range as your tax burden. If you take losses in your early years, you can use them to offset future earnings.

The final item on the expense side is professional services. In the modern era of outsourcing, this is important.

If you're hiring attorneys, accountants, management consultants, outsourced CFOs, etc., they have an hourly, daily, weekly or monthly cost. Our model uses a daily rate, and then we forecast how many days per month we'll need those services.

> There is this tendency to just lunge into business without a careful study of the market, customers, and competition.

The beauty of having all your revenue and expense assumptions in one place is that you can run scenario analyses to see how your business is impacted by certain events. What if you only get half the expected bookings? What if the cost of insurance or employee costs go way up? You can test these things to see how seriously your bottom line will be impacted.

Volume & Pricing Estimates

Many entrepreneurs struggle with the concept of how to set pricing. There are a lot of schools of thought here. Some base pricing on the competitive landscape. Others set it based on a factor of cost with an acceptable "profit" added on top. Still others base their pricing on the value to the customer.

Honestly, it pays to do some research across all fronts in order to give yourself some clarity about how you intend to fit into the marketplace.

Competing on price is often a serious mistake. If competitive pressure is driving you to set your prices, is there really room in your market for your business? Is there more you can do in delivering your goods or services to differentiate yourself and thereby break free of the bonds of competitive

> Getting involved in low-priced competition is generally a race to the bottom and a good way to destroy a business.

pricing? Getting involved in low-priced competition is generally a race to the bottom and a good way to destroy a business.

Knowledge of your cost base is certainly wise in helping you avoid situations where you lose money. And this isn't just a factor of your Cost of Goods Sold (COGS) but also all of the operating expenses of your business. You want to sell at a price that leads you to overall profitability. Here, having a full-fledged financial model can help you play with various scenarios to see what happens when you change your pricing. If you raise prices, how much faster do you reach profitability (your breakeven point)? If you lower prices, what happens to your model?

It's worth noting here that many entrepreneurs let their personal hang ups get in the way of their pricing decisions. Phrases like "I don't want to be too greedy," or "my customers can't afford that" or "no one will pay that" creep into the thought process, and it's usually a huge mistake. Perceived customer value is much more important, and pricing sets a strong signal about your company.

You don't have to serve everyone, either. Think about it, would you rather have 1,000 customers paying you $100 for something, or 25 customers paying you $10,000? Many people think in terms of having the most possible customers, but that's not always the most profitable answer. The reality is that it's much easier to serve those fewer customers well and reinforce your value proposition.

Going back to our NeurTours example, let's say I go out and I do market research, and I find out that there are 100,000 people in the United States who subscribe to an outdoor adventure magazine like *Adventure Cyclist* and also own their own business. They are prime candidates for what I do.

Then I can narrow that down further and find adventurous business owners who have revenues of at least $1 million. From there, I build a list, and I estimate that 2% of those people will opt into something I'm doing online or a direct mail piece that shows their interest in my company. That's two thousand people in my database who have raised their hands.

So, when an Investor says, "Well, how do you know that you're going to get 30 people to pay you $10,000 to go on these trips? It's because I've gone out, done research, have gotten potential customers to respond who appreciate my value proposition, and I know these people have income above a certain level such that they can easily afford something like this. And, I know their existing interests already align with what I'm doing.

Benefits of the Financial Model

Once you've developed all of your assumptions, that drive your forward-looking forecast, what's the benefit to you?

For starters, you're going to know how much capital you're going to need to survive throughout the course of the forecast period. The number one cause of business failure is a lack of capital.

> The number one cause of business failure is a lack of capital.

Carefully thinking out your model, with realistic conservative assumptions, will help you understand when and how much capital you are likely to need to keep everything moving forward. This is incredibly valuable information that lets you plan far in advance versus having to scramble around at the last minute trying to find resources, for which you'll likely have to pay a lot more.

Another huge benefit is giving you a valuation of what your business is worth in today's dollars, if you hit all the goals and milestones laid out in your plan. How many people appear on *Shark Tank* without the slightest clue of what their business is worth? How many existing business owners operate their business with forward-looking targets and an understanding of what their business is worth? Not many.

Scenario analysis is another massive benefit to modeling that allows you to "see the future" if certain things happen. Many entrepreneurs model best case, worst case, and most likely scenarios to give themselves a sense of all of the possibilities. How bad would things look under the absolute worst outcome? What happens if you significantly exceed your expected outcomes? The value of this kind of thoughtful analysis is priceless and can lead you to better decision making.

Turning your forecast into graphics can also be super helpful in visualizing what is happening in the business. Whether you're presenting this information to investors or as part of your own key performance indicator (KPI) dashboard, it's great to be able to quickly grasp what's going on by looking at a chart.

It can also be helpful to split your business into various departments. You may have a General & Admin department, Sales & Marketing, Operations, and Research & Development. Each department may have its own specific set of costs, including employees, and segregating them allows you to forecast what's happening specific to each function of your business.

In the case of NeurTours, there's really not a lot of heavy cash requirements because I'm going to require most of my participants to put down a pretty sizable deposit before I go out and pay other vendors. So the capital needs of the business are low and I don't have to go out and raise huge amounts from investors.

For about $25,000, I can go out and create my website, do my marketing, plan my first trip, fill it up, and the business is fully launched. It makes sense to hold off on major capital purchases until I successfully run the first trip. If I must rent equipment the first go round, so be it.

Once fully established, it will be easier to do so then. Your venture may be much more capital intensive, require substantial hiring, or have a long development cycle. That's OK, most businesses are. Your financial model allows you to understand when you'll need those capital infusions in your business.

Cash flow management is also a big benefit of modeling. Watching your cash flows and making sure that your cash balance always has a healthy reserve and that your company has enough "runway" to survive to profitability is mission critical.

Another benefit to modeling is helping you look at debt versus equity scenarios, if you decide you're going to raise capital. Debt means you don't have to give up ownership in your company, but you have to "service" the debt in the form of monthly or quarterly payments, which can hurt your cash flows. On the flip side, equity investors don't generally expect to get paid from the cash flows of the business, but they do become co-owners in the company, which can be fantastic in some situations, but a nightmare in others. Whenever possible, pick equity investors who can add more than just cash to your business.

For NeurTours, here's what my model tells me about the business:

NeurTours Net Present Valuation							
Investment		Year 1	Year 2	Year 3	Year 4	Year 5	Terminal Value
	($25,000)	$62,485	$200,202	$301,343	$555,516	$851,395	$5,675,968
Net Present Value			$3,573,643				
Internal Rate of Return			394%				
Weighted Average Cost of Capital			15.00%				

I can see from this valuation that I will be marginally profitable in year one, and that overall, the net present valuation is above $3.5 million. For me, this isn't a full-time venture, but a fun side business, from which I am likely to draw just as much wisdom and inspiration from my participants as they are from me.

Maybe two years from now, someone comes to me and asks if I'd like to sell this business. I already know from my initial modeling what the business was worth when I started it. I may want to update my model and see if that number has changed significantly.

The Financial Model - It's all in the Details

A five-year forecast is going to have 60 months' worth of data, 20 quarters, and five years. That's quite a bit of data. Drilling down to that level of detail may be a bit of over-kill but having this information in the early going can he extremely helpful, particularly so you can get a sense of your monthly "burn rate" or how much expense you incur while you are getting your company up and running. The reality of most companies, particularly in the early going, is that business is going to ramp up from zero, versus showing level sales throughout the first year. Other companies may have a cyclical sales cycle.

In the case of NeurTours, I might be more active in the summer months, when the weather is nicer in the Northern Hemisphere (although that doesn't preclude me from running something on the far side of the world). You want to take these things into account, particularly in the first year or two. Likewise, you probably won't hire every new employee on January 1st, and you may want to push off some of that salary expense until it's critical to bring people on.

Most people tend to gravitate towards the income statement when it comes to financial forecasting, but attention should also be paid to the balance sheet and cash flow forecasts, as they are also extremely important parts of any accounting system. Here at Blue Horizon Venture Consulting, we actually model out three kinds of cash flow statements - a standard Financial Accounting Standards Board (FASB) format, a Receipts and Disbursements format, and a cash Sources and Uses format. They should all result in the same number, and it's great to be able to cross check them against each other to make sure they end up with the same cash balance at the end. If not, the model has a problem.

Yes, finance and accounting are not the most exciting things in the world for most people. But they are so very critical, and in my nearly a quarter century of working with early-stage companies, it is one of the most prevalent weaknesses I see, and it's the one that most often gets entrepreneurs into trouble. I've worked with some amazing visionary people who were great fun to be around with amazing energy and plans, but who just absolutely lacked any sort of financial acumen, and their plans completely unraveled when they inevitably ran into financial troubles. This could have been prevented with foresight and planning. The resulting fallout is not pretty to watch. It's sad to see.

In the world of outsourced services, make sure you account for any outside help you're going to require, whether it's a development team, attorneys, accountants, consultants, etc. Make sure you've accounted for any large expenditures along the way - new equipment, or new space that you might need as your operation grows. In short, think forward.

Financial Model Final Thoughts

When I do consulting work for my early-stage, high-growth clients, financial modeling is one of the first things I do. It leads to critical thinking that often has been neglected in favor of short-term realities, and it's usually a helpful and eye-opening process for my clients. I'm proud of the base model we use at BHVC and the fact that it can be customized for pretty much any situation.

I should pause here to talk about canned business plan software. There are some good programs out there for business plan development, but they all have limitations, and one of the bigger ones I've seen is the inability to show assumptions in one place that can easily been manipulated to run scenarios. Some flat out just don't show you where assumptions came from and how the founders arrived at them. Still others have major limitations on customization. I much prefer to build out my models in Excel with the "open canvas" it represents, and once done, I might transfer my data into a canned software program. They can be an excellent tool for benchmarking and ongoing management of a business plan, once complete.

It's funny, when I watch Shark Tank, I can generally tell within a few minutes which entrepreneurs have done financial modeling and which haven't. While I do understand and have seen people who suffer from "analysis paralysis," the complete lack of planning can be just as debilitating. Over the course of my career, the clients who get and understand the financials underpinning their businesses have been much more successful.

There's a study out of Stanford University that shows one of the leading predictive factors of success for startup businesses is whether or not they have gone through the process, just the process, of business planning. Another study out of Virginia Tech found that people who write down their goals earned nine times the income over their lifetime. Nine times! Isn't that worth the effort?

3

MARKET RESEARCH

Introduction to Market Research

> There is this tendency to just lunge into business without a careful study of the market, customers, and competition.

Another area I see many entrepreneurs fall short is in conducting market research. There is this tendency to just lunge into business without a careful study of the market, customers, and competition. Even with existing businesses, there is a general lack of knowledge about what's going on in their own industry and their local market. They tend to operate in their own bubble, and often get surprised to find out that things have shifted around them. In this digital era where change comes with increasing speed, not staying on top of this is a mistake. Business owners may soon find the market and the industry has left them far behind.

Fear not, access to information has made this a lot easier than it was even at the end of the 20th century. I can recall doing research for projects that actually required me to go to this thing called a library, and pull thick, voluminous things called books off of shelves and then leaf through hundreds and hundreds of pages to find things like industry multiples. Now, you can ask Alexa. And really, Artificial Intelligence (AI) will likely make it easier and easier to stay on top of what's happening.

The things you want to know are generally the size of your market, details on the market niches that you might be in, what trends have been in the markets the last couple of years, what is forecasted to happen in the future, everything you can find out about your target customers, and who your main competitors are and how they operate.

The Market Research Framework

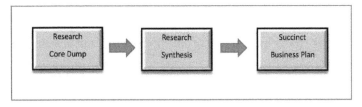

I have always followed a process that I would recommend, as research can quickly get out of control. Assuming the bulk of your research will be done online (but don't forget your primary research of actually talking to potential customers!), it's a good idea to create folders on your hard drive for your research and any subcategories you want to use. As you find reports and documents relating to your subject, quickly scan then, and if they appear relevant, dump then into your folder system. Don't get hung up in reading everything. Your first pass is just to gather as much as you can, your "core dump."

In the case of articles, I personally like to create a Word document, for my example, "NeurTours Research," and simply cut and paste all of the articles into that document.

After I have exhausted all the sources we'll discuss shortly, I then synthesize that information into relevant data. Here I'm taking perhaps hundreds, if not thousands of pages of information and condensing it into perhaps a few dozen pages of the most pertinent info.

Then, I'm ready to write those sections of my business plan, even further condensing those pages into the most relative, hard-hitting facts that support my business model and financial forecast.

Frankly, this can be the most time-consuming part of the entire business plan process, but the information you gain is priceless as you build your strategic plans. And when you understand what's happening, you're able to answer questions your investors or key stakeholders might have that prove you know your stuff.

This intel can also indicate where some of your financial assumptions may be off, and you can go back and adjust accordingly. In fact, you can drive your assumptions off your market data, by showing that you expect to capture a certain percentage of market share over time. Presenting your assumptions in this light lends credibility to them and makes them much, much easier to defend.

Free Sources of Market Research

One thing's for sure, I am glad I'm not in the industry of selling market research. It is getting harder and harder to protect such work in an era of increasing freedom of information. And with the coming advances in 5G technology, it won't be long before the entire world has access to vast quantities of information at their fingertips. The problem of the future, in fact, may not be lack of available information, but having access to too much of it, and not being able to process or synthesize it.

One of the first steps you'll want to take is to create some sort of system for collecting information. I think back to one of the first plans I ever wrote, when I was still a business school student at UCLA. I was there during the height of the Dot Com era, which was a really exciting time to be there with the rise of the Internet and technology. I remember fellow students being all fired up about their Palm Pilots and being able to transmit business card data from device to device wirelessly. Seems like the Stone Age just over 20 years later.

One of my first clients was one of the first ever online mortgage companies. I printed hundreds and hundreds of pages of articles on the industry and remember sitting in my living room surrounded by piles of them, organizing them into categories and then working through them all to whittle down all of this information into something succinct and usable in a business plan.

Now that most things are digital, you can set up a few file folders on your computer and just cut, paste, and save all the data you could want. Just make sure your files are backed up, or you could inadvertently lose a lot of work that you must go back and repeat.

In the case with NeurTours, I'm doing research on adventure travel. But I'm also trying to do some research on mastermind groups and how many there are out there, etc.

The obvious first stop are Google's search engine. There are other search engines out there, but like it or not, they pale in comparison. One of the first things you'll want to do is enter your industry name followed by key phrases like "market size," "market forecast," "market trends," "statistics," etc. Use quotations if your phrase has two or more words, so that Google knows you are searching for that whole phrase, and not just the first word in that phrase.

On my first pass, I'm just skimming a few words then either saving articles into my folder or cutting and pasting into a Word doc, and most likely both. Remember to save your sources and cite them, always, especially when using direct quotes, graphics, or data. You may get asked where you got your information, and it's always good to have an answer.

You can really get lost down a rabbit hole on research, so the key here is to just compile it quickly. You can go back and read it and narrow it all down later. At the end of the day, the hundreds, or even thousands of pages of information you collect are going to get narrowed down to perhaps 3-4 pages of concise information - the most relevant facts and figures for the business plan.

This process is what I call a "core dump." Just find anything and everything you can in your industry. Depending on your industry, you should do quite well. Once you've exhausted some of the keyword phrases, you can try looking for industry associations and publications. Some of these reports or sites require you to join or pay, but if you get the exact title of their publications and then enter the exact title into a Google search, sometimes you can find it republished elsewhere for free, and other times it may lead you to an article that quotes that report, which could be at least, if not more, valuable.

In the case of NeurTours, I found a publication called *Adventure Travel News*. Right away, I see they compile industry data and that they have a $100 billion market. That tells me there's a lot of spending in my space. I see they also have some very cool reports with a minimal cost, but that are free to members. They also have a free membership, so I join and then I get free access to their rather extensive reports.

Most reports have a section about the authors. These could be people you reach out to directly. You could ask them for additional information or to point you in the direction of more resources. You could even ask them if they'd be interested in serving as advisors to your company. Most of the time, researchers would be very flattered by this.

In the case of the adventure travel market, there is more data than I could ever possibly want. Having done research for hundreds and hundreds of clients, I know that's not always the case. Specialized niche markets or highly technical markets tend to have more closely guarded data.

What I find in my research on NeurTours is that there are some niches within the adventure travel market that I might want to dig into. They have "hard" and "soft" segments, which are the difference between, say, climbing a mountain or cycling across the country, and more sedentary pursuits, like birdwatching. So that helps me further understand my market.

I also find a lot of companies whose brands are well recognized by adventure travelers, like REI and Patagonia. There may be some advertising possibilities with these companies to tap into some of their customer base.

The next thing I find is a list of the top magazines being read by adventure travelers in the U. S. What a great list to find! That's 10 places I can advertise because I know adventure travelers are reading them. A lot of the reports you find will lead you to other sources of information. It's like following the proverbial trail of breadcrumbs.

What's most interesting to me is that I find that the "hard travel" segment is much smaller, about ten times smaller than the soft travel segment.

I can them look at other ways to slice and dice my market. Looking at global geographic segments, it shows that North Americans make up the largest segment of hard travel adventurers. So right away, I'm thinking that when I market to US and Canadian prospects, doing something rigorous might be more appealing, but if I decide to do tours in other parts of the world, maybe I should dial it back a little on the difficulty scale. Nothing wrong with a week on a faraway pristine beach!

I find other information about average trip lengths, average spending per trip, etc. I want to price as a premium experience, but it makes sense to understand customer alternatives as well.

One of the bits of information I found, is that in the North American market, soft adventure customers pay twice as much as hard adventure customers. Hmm, that sort of turns some of my logic on its head. So, while I originally started my thinking that leading a mountain climbing trip or a cycling adventure was the way to go, now my market research is starting to lead me in a different direction. I can't let my personal bias and preference creep in here, I need to go with proven data.

I dig a little deeper into how people research their trips. It shows that more than 80% are researching trips online. So online advertising is going to be important.

I further found information about the Baby Boomers and how they are awakening to the adventure travel experience. They're probably going to be wanting to do something lower key, and that's certainly important. That said, I met a cycling friend of mine and his group as they were completing their cross-country trip from San Diego to St. Augustine. One of the people on the tour was an 80-year-old man who had pedaled the whole way. He had lost his wife a few years earlier and had been in a funk, but his son convinced him to do this tour, and it really changed his attitude. He had tears streaming down his face as we entered St. Augustine. So, I can't discount this segment, nor should I discount the ability of people to participate in adventure travel, even at older ages. Some older folks are even starting new businesses after retiring, as "encore careers." After all, if you retire at 65, and live past 100, that's a long time where you can accomplish a lot with a lot of wisdom. So maybe I consider targeting a senior group that fits this category, with a trip that is a little less physical and more cerebral.

> So few go through this exercise and just proceed to build their business through the lens of their own bias or intuition.

See how the market research can lead you in new directions? So sad that so few go through this exercise and just proceed to build their business through the lens of their own bias or intuition. Often, it's flat out wrong for their intended market. Had I launched into this without research, I very likely would have fallen into that trap.

I also find out about some big industry conferences and trade shows that I might want to attend. Knowing my customers are also entrepreneurs, I need to think about events where I can get in front of entrepreneurs who have disposable income. If they can attend a $5000 conference and spend another $3000 on travel to get to and stay there, they are in my wheelhouse.

The further you can niche your research, the better. My goal is to come up with reasonable assumptions for my financial forecast, but I am also looking ahead to how I am going to market to and attract my customers. In this case, I know that Facebook and list brokers are going to be my friends. In either case, it's easy to specifically target business owners who are interested in adventure travel.

With the list brokers, maybe I ask for the list of business owners who subscribe to *Entrepreneur* magazine and a relevant adventure travel magazine. I could even further target by the type of trip I want to run. Let's say I want to do a cycling trip. Then I get the list of *Entrepreneur* and *Adventure Cycling* subscribers. Same for an over 50 or over 65 tour. Bingo, not only does the size of my requested list give me good information about the potential size of my market, but when I'm ready to pull the trigger, I have people totally predisposed to what I have to offer.

I'll say it again, just for the point of re-emphasis, cite your sources. In fact, write them into your business plan. For example:

> "According to research done by the Adventure Travel Trade Association, in 2020, one out of every four travelers likes……"

Citing source in this way is not only the right thing to do, but it shows investors and stakeholders that you've done your homework and you understand your market and industry. So yes, all those awful book reports you had to do in school did have a purpose!

I don't want to neglect the other side of my business which is business masterminding. It's a practice that has gained significant momentum over the years, particularly in the past 20, because of the work of author Napoleon Hill of *Think and Grow Rich* fame.

This is a little tougher to research, and some of you may find yourselves in similar situations. Heck, you may even have an entirely new product or service. I couldn't find data about masterminds, but I did find a company that has mastermind group facilitator training, and this lady is probably going to be a huge resource when I start talking to her.

In fact, she may be able to provide me with some leads for people who can serve as my trip leaders in the future. And perhaps she has some sources of data that I don't know about.

Here's another good point - as you do your research, keep tabs on people, groups, and companies that might make good joint venture partners. Even though I have participated in multiple masterminds and have facilitated one of my own, I will take this training. Another benefit of having done this work!

Paid Sources of Research

There are, of course, plenty of paid sources of market research. Hoovers.com is a source of private company information, and they have compiled research on many private companies out there. Dun & Bradstreet does as well. MarketResearch.com, and First Research are just a few other examples where you can find good research. LexisNexis is a great tool to use if you're searching magazines and periodicals for relevant articles about your industry. Sometimes you can get samples of the first few pages of these reports, which might give you all the high-level data you need.

If you know an attorney, most of them have access to LexisNexis when they're doing legal research. So, perhaps you can access their system. Or your local library or nearby university library may have some database access, although the latter is generally reserved for students and faculty. Sometimes you can purchase a community access pass, which could be a lot less expensive than are the reports.

Forrester is a big research group in IT and the technical fields. If you happen to be involved in health care, maybe Forrester Research might have some good information for you as well.

Economist Intelligence Unit it an amazing source when you're thinking about expanding internationally. It has intelligence about specific countries and doing business in each.

Business Insights is another great research tool, but, it's expensive. I was part of a group that subscribed to it for a while, but we didn't get enough use out of it to justify the cost. It was amazing for some industries and not as helpful on others.

Introduction to Customer & Competitive Intelligence

Once you're drilled down into your industry and market, past, present and future, it's time to start digging for details on your customers and competitors.

I used to work in competitive intelligence in the health care industry, so I did tons and tons of research on the competitors and potential acquisition candidates for Blue Cross and Blue Shield of Florida (now Florida Blue) and learned to dig up a lot of dirt on the competition. My focus was on financial metrics and enrollment numbers, but I also looked at employment and job openings - other metrics that gave an indication of the health of competitors.

For public companies, information is abundant as it's required by law in 10Q (quarterly reports) and 10K (annual reports) with the SEC. Most public companies also publish their own annual reports. Most companies also publish a fair amount of detail about themselves on their own websites to attract customers, which can be very helpful. And again, there's Hoovers and Dun & Bradstreet if all else fails.

With customers, you want to find demographic information like people's age, their income, psychographic information which includes hobbies, their likes, their attitudes, and their dislikes.

Doing this research and understanding who your customers are, helps you tell the story about how you're going to find customers, attract them to you, and turn them into revenue.

By the way, all businesses have competition, either direct competitors or substitutes for what you do or sell. The worst mistake you can make in a business plan is to tell people you don't have any competition because it's just flat out not true. Investors will run, not walk, if you utter the words "we don't have any competition."

There's always some kind of substitute for what you're doing, so keep that in mind. I know a lot of people that have innovative new products think that way but there's always a substitute out there in some way, shape or form. So, you need to make sure you understand that and include that kind of information in your plan.

Demographics

Let's do just a little deeper dive into the topic of Demographics. Here are some of the sources I use to get a better handle on this topic:

Census.gov - The census happens in the United States every 10 years. In fact, it's going on right now in 2020 as I write this, and the latest data will be released by the end of March 2021. The Census attempts to account for every person in the country, and specific details about where they live, what they do, etc. You can download tables that let you slice and dice population data in many different ways - age, sex, location, income, education, race, etc. The Census also provides "Statistics of U.S. Businesses," or SUSB, which gives you interesting data on the business side of the ledger. This business data is updated more frequently. The nice thing is, you can segment by industry and really drill down into what's happening in your particular industry by NAICS code. If you don't know the NAICS code for your industry, you can look it up at www.naics.com and then use that code in your SUSB search.

IRS.gov - This is particularly relevant if you're doing B to B type business where you're selling to other companies. If you do a search on "industries" from within the IRS site, you'll find links to some pretty good resources. You may have to hunt a little, but it's there. Some of this is industry information put together by the IRS for their own internal auditors who were auditing businesses so that they would understand the industries. But you can come in here and use that same information to understand the industries better yourself

Fedstats.gov/Data.gov - Fedstats.gov was an excellent source of data that got compiled from over 100 different federal agencies. It seems to have disappeared around 2018. Perhaps it will be revived one day.

Bureau of Labor Statistics (www.bls.gov) - Let's say you're trying to estimate wage costs for your financial model. On your first pass, you sort of guesstimated. Now, you want to get a little more accurate. You can look up average earnings by industry. You click on this and you can find out the average salaries in your industry, and perhaps you want to model yours slightly higher so that you can attract the best talent. You can drill down to specifics by county, get data on inflation, consumer price index numbers, etc. A treasure trove of job-related data.

Zip Code Demographics - There used to be a great tool called ZipSkinny, but it's no longer operable. There are tools like Melissa.com, and CDXTech.com, and while they give some useful information, they seemed designed to perhaps draw you in to pay for other services. These sites tend to shift, so just search the term "zip code demographics" and you should get some applicable sites that will provide you with some data. This is especially useful if your customer target market is very localized.

Info USA - This is a very comprehensive source of mailing lists, but you can use their data to help understand your market. Let's say you're a dentist. You want to know the number of dentists in your market area under the age of 50. InfoUSA can tell you how many there are. You get to decide if you want to pay them for their list of contacts. They have 15 million businesses in their databases and more than 200 million consumers.

In my case with NeurTours, I find out that there are 22,000 people in the 35-55 age range in my close geographic market area with an income of greater than $100,000 who also own a business, and subscribe to one or more magazines on adventure travel. I know this is a pretty darn good match for the types of people that might make excellent customers for NeurTours. Maybe I can narrow that down even further to people with CEO, President, or Founder in their title. The more laser focused I am, the better I can have a message and media match that will resonate with those folks!

With all this research done, perhaps I can start to make some sort of market penetration expectation that says I will capture 1-2% of them as customers. In my case, I only need a handful of customers at a time, and the ideal scenario is that I have a waiting list and have created a demand issue whereby I might need to expand operations and/or charge more.

Bottom line is, when you have done this level of detailed research, you truly are in a more defensible position with investors and other stakeholders in terms of being able to reach your goals and milestones.

Psychographics

Perhaps at least as important as demographics, but less understood, are psychographics. Here, we're talking about

> The values, attitudes, interests and lifestyles of your customers.

the values, attitudes, interests and lifestyles of your customers. You're getting inside their heads and understanding who they are, and what they're all about. This helps you understand how you might be able to relate to them. Not only is this a strong signal to investors that you know and understand your customers, but it's going to help you immensely in your marketing.

It's also going to help you understand how you might further segment your market and drill down with your demographic assumptions. And as you saw with Info USA, and with advertisers like Facebook, there were some hobbies and other things that you could plug in that could further narrow down your focus.

Customer validation is very important. Anybody you talk to is going to want to make sure that whatever you're selling, whether a good or a service, is going to have a market for people to buy it. You may find some studies and reports that show your product or service is already generally accepted. That shouldn't be too difficult to come by because you have existing sales in your industry that you can focus on.

One of the best things you can do is create a survey, and surveying is a way to really get direct firsthand empirical evidence supporting your idea. It may also tell you that your idea is somewhat off base. That's not necessarily a bad thing. You may have to back up and think again about what you're doing and if you have the right products and services, if you're getting negative feedback. Survey Monkey offers both free and paid surveys that you can create and distribute quickly.

In my case, Survey Monkey already had a vacation travel template, which meant all I had to do was tweak a few of the questions to suit my company and I was ready to go. If you look for industry specific templates, you may find one that will save you some time. You can gauge interest in your concept and how much people are willing to pay through the questions you ask. Be careful not to ask leading questions as it can skew your results.

Once you create a survey, you simply get a link to it and email it out to groups of people who fit your customer profile, or you post it on pages where these people congregate, such as Facebook groups or LinkedIn groups. You may need to offer some sort of incentive, like a Starbucks gift card or an Amazon card, or perhaps even something free from your company, which can start you on the road to building a customer list. It will be money well spent. Alumni groups and industry groups to which you belong might also make good places to ask for responses. Some entrepreneurs will even grab a clipboard and go out and talk to real live actual people. In my situation, an airport might be a good place to find adventure travelers. Get creative!

> Some entrepreneurs will even grab a clipboard and go out and talk to real live actual people.

Once you dial in your offer and get positive feedback, you can plug these results right into your plan. You can create some charts and graphs from this research that tells you exactly what your customers are thinking. It's impressive to do this, but few entrepreneurs are willing to take the time to do this work, so if you do, you'll stand out. And it's essentially free, aside from the investment of your time.

Competitive Intelligence

One of the worst things you can ever state in your business plan is that you have no competition. The chances of this being true are extremely small, and even if by some miracle it is true, just don't state it. Investors will immediately write you off.

Understanding your competition is extremely important. A huge amount of data can be gleaned from the Internet. Type in your industry name, and if you're a local business, your market area. A list of existing competitors will pop up.

When I did research for NeurTours, which has a global market, I found a report that said there were 139 operators in the UK. So right away I know there are likely thousands worldwide.

Once you have the name of a couple of your competitors, you can often find a list of other competitors by simply scrolling to the bottom of a Google search and looking at the "searches related to" section that shows what other sites people have searched related to that one. It's a good way to start building your competitor list. Another is to simply search for "Company X competitors," company X of course being the name of your competitor.

For NeurTours, I found a company called Maverick Business Adventures. Interesting group and checking out their website and offerings gives me some ideas about how I might want to position NeurTours. That's probably the closest direct competitor, although I also have to consider that anyone running Mastermind groups, or anyone running adventure tours, for that matter, are substitutes for the NeurTours offering that my target customers might choose as alternatives.

Another thing you want to research here are industry trade shows. If your business is region-specific, you want to look for region-specific industry trade shows. Find out who is exhibiting and sponsoring those trade shows, and you'll likely discover a few competitors.

You might also want to run a patent search at the US Patent and Trademark website, uspto.gov, where you can find inventors and companies that hold patents in your industry. This can sometimes be a great way to discover competitors, but also the founders who started them. You may also find some things that those companies and inventors have not yet rolled out to the market. This can be extremely helpful in anticipating what your competitors may soon be up to.

Once you have a solid list of competitors, you want to search Google News for their names. This will give you the latest and greatest information on what they've been up to, if newsworthy.

And of course, companies love to brag about their own accomplishments on their very own websites, particularly if they use their sites to actively sell to customers. As such, you may find helpful information that is published nowhere else, right on their website - sales statistics, client names, testimonials,

There are also sites like Alexa.com and Compete.com that give you information on website traffic that you can use as a barometer of how well your competitors are doing online. That said, just because a competitor is or isn't doing well online, does not necessarily mean they aren't winning or losing overall. Some competitors just might be doing different forms of marketing such as radio, television, newspaper, or magazine and not necessarily doing tons of pay per click or other online promotion.

When I build a competitive section for my business plans, I generally build a big table. I'll have three columns, the name, address, and phone number of the competitors in the left column, the website and traffic in the middle column, and then in the third column, their pricing and product offerings, revenues - and any interesting information I can find.

Public companies are super easy. Yahoo Finance is a great source of high-level data for your public companies, the ones that are traded on the stock market. Freeedgar. com and SEC.gov are great sources for 10Q's and 10K's required every quarter and every year, respectively. It's all public information so you can download these reports, and a lot of times they will have great information about your industry and specifically about your competitors and what they're doing.

Again, Hoovers and Dun and Bradstreet (D&B) are paid sources of info on private companies. They won't have micro companies, but they do have a fairly extensive database of every company that has trade credit of any kind.

I also like to write a paragraph in the business plan for the top competitors, just describing what's going on with them and why my company is positioned differently or better than they are. Investors want to make sure that you understand what the competitive marketplace looks like and how you are positioned within that marketplace.

4

THE BUSINESS PLAN

The Business Plan Outline

OK, the research is done, and honestly, that is usually the most time-consuming part of the process - hunting, gathering, reading, sorting, and synthesizing the data about your industry, your market, your customers, and your competitors is no small task, so congratulations!

Here, we want to just take a quick look at each of the sections in your business plan, and then in subsequent sections, we'll dive into each in more detail.

Cover Page - If you haven't already created a logo for your business, it's a good idea, and something that can be done very inexpensively. Sites like Fiverr.com or Hatchwise.com are just two examples of places where you can get graphic designers to create something for you for anywhere from a few dollars, to a few hundred. This seemingly minor detail lets people know that you're invested into your business and that you have a real going concern. Of course, if you've been in business for a while, you likely already have this done. It adds a level of professionalism to your plan. Honestly, not having one, or having a cheap-looking logo, can leave the opposite impression.

Table of Contents - Microsoft Word and other word processing programs generally have excellent Table of Contents features that allow you to organize the content of your plan. They are also generally linkable, meaning that if a reader clicks on a heading in your table, they can quickly jump to the section of the plan they want to see. This is extremely helpful. If you don't know how to manage headings and tables of contents, there are some great tutorial videos on YouTube and elsewhere, or within the help sections of the software itself. You should also familiarize yourself with Style Sheets, which can help you maintain a uniform appearance throughout your plan. There's nothing worse than reading a plan that has different fonts, different font sizes and different indentations. To a reader, it sort of signals a possible lack of organization that might exist within your company, and it's not a message you want to convey. Within Word, if you hit the PF9 or F9 key on your keyboard, the table of contents will update after you've made additional changes. A good reader experience should not be overlooked when building your plan. It can be very frustrating to have to hunt for certain information, and like it or not, most readers who get your plan, will either jump around or skim it, before deciding if they want to dive in.

The Executive Summary is the first thing you see in a business plan, but is generally the last thing you write, once all the detail is in place. Write it as if it's a standalone document, because often, you'll want to carve it off and use it as a "teaser" to see if people are interested, before disclosing all your info to them.

It should be a heavy-hitting piece that will engage the reader. A lot of people that you're going to deal with - from bankers to venture capitalists to angel investors or even friends and family - they're going to want to quickly digest your idea without having to read a 20+ page document.

> The idea of the Executive Summary is to capture their attention and hopefully get them to dig further into the plan.

The idea of the Executive Summary is

to capture their attention and hopefully get them to dig further into the plan.

Financial Model - this isn't a separate section per se, but it's worth noting here that a picture can be worth a lot of words. Creating graphs and charts of your financial model can show in a quick graphic what might otherwise take paragraphs to explain. As such, they are real space savers, and can also be helpful to readers who ingest information visually versus being forced to read for it. It's best to present both and let people kind of pick and choose how they want to digest the information.

Likewise, an organization chart in your management section can be a powerful way to show your organization, or perhaps more likely, your FUTURE organization. Microsoft PowerPoint can create a variety of org charts, and of course there are other software tools out there that can do the same, or better. Once done, you can simply cut and paste it into your plan.

Disclaimer - You always need to be careful if you're using a plan to raise capital, particularly when you're raising equity capital. There are a lot of laws having to do with securities and you want to make sure that you are not getting sideways with the SEC or any other governmental agency. So, some basic language here that says you are not soliciting, that your plan is for information only, etc. is wise. If you visit www.BrassTacksBooks.com/WWBP you can download a sample disclaimer to model. It's up to you whether you get recipients to sign this page. As a rule, asking investors or others to sign NDAs or anything else for that matter, is going to cut down significantly on the number of people who actually do look at it.

Long Term Vision -This is a little bonus section that we include in the executive summary. If there are things you may want to accomplish in your business in the future, but they just don't fit into the five-year financial forecast window of your plan, here's your chance to talk about those goals and show readers that you have a clear vision for the future of your business.

Market Opportunity - This is the section where you synthesize all of that research you've done into a succinct, hard-hitting summary of what's happening in your market and industry. Again, always cite sources when using charts, graphs, and data. You generally want to keep this to three or four pages, so resist the temptation to go overboard. As the old police saying goes, "Just the facts, ma'am" (or man).

Products & Intellectual Property - Here you want to describe your products and services in great detail, show pictures where appropriate, and discuss any sort of IP you possess that might give you a competitive advantage and a defensible position in the market, be it trademarks, patents, or trade secrets (which of course you won't disclose, but merely mention).

Customers and Competition - Once again, a chance to share your research, show you've carefully analyzed the space in which you'll operate, and give readers a good sense that you have a good market position.

Operating Plan - Goals and milestones, where you're going to be located, logistics, materials, and product flows, fulfillment, customer service. These are all bases you want to cover in this section. If you have an existing location, put up a picture. Show a map of your location. Create timelines on what you plan to accomplish and when. In essence, you're showcasing your implementation goals.

Marketing & Sales Plan - Many people make the mistake of glossing over this section. To many investors and stakeholders, this is the most important section of your plan. You can have the absolute best product or service on the planet, but if you lack the ability to attract customers, your business is likely to fail.

Management and Advisers - This is where you can showcase your team, whether you're a company with hundreds of employees, or a solopreneur, you're still going to have a team around you. Some of it could be your advisors - formal or informal. Your attorney, CPA, consultant, website developer, or virtual assistant are all part of your team. No entrepreneur is an island.

Financial Plan - Of course you have your full set of financials built out over five years, right? Here is where you'll want to verbalize and summarize that model, and current and past results as well, if you have them.

Appendices - You can include technical details, and any other data that you otherwise don't want to have clutter up your plan. One of the things we always include to lead off this section is a subsection on risks and mitigating factors.

It's a good idea to lay these all out in plain sight. Lawyers love this because it's all about disclosure. If someone comes back to you later and accuses you of not disclosing something to them, you're covered if you included it here.

So now let's start to dig into each of the sections in more detail.

The Product/Service Section

Here's is where you want to tell the story of your products or services and what your company is all about. Be factual about it, without being too salesy. I've seen a lot of poorly written plans just fill this section with a bunch of sales copy, and that generally won't help the cause.

For NeurTours, I have a couple of my initial tours planned out. One is a bicycle tour from Ft. Lauderdale down through the Keys to Key West, ferry up to Ft. Meyers Beach, and then a ride back across "Alligator Alley" to the starting point. Another is climbing Mt. Kilimanjaro in Tanzania. So, I might give descriptions of those tours, share the itineraries, and show my pricing.

I will also give a description of one of our long week-end tours. We have a cycling tour that runs from Amelia Island, Florida, down to St. Augustine, and back up the St. John's River to the Jacksonville airport.

You want to showcase your products, explain why they are unique, how they solve your customer need, desire, and/or pain. You want to explain this in a narrative, engaging way. Use pictures, animation, drawings, anything that really describes what your products or services are all about. If you have a complex set of products/services, you can list them in a table. This is often helpful, especially if you have a large number of SKUs or product items. You don't want to get overly complicated. Break things into summary groupings if your offerings are super complicated. You can always add appendices at the end of the plan for more detail. Be concise and effective here.

You also want to include your pricing. It may be a price range if you're grouping into categories. Where do you fit in the market? Are you the lowest price in the market? Do you have the best quality? Are you offering products to a certain niche of people? What's your position?

You'll also want to discuss technology and intellectual property. If you're in a high-tech type of business, this is going to be critical. What are the platforms and tech tools your company is using?

Does your company possess any intellectual property (IP)? U.S. patent filings, international patent filings, or trademarks are examples of IP. If you have a really cool logo, are trying to protect a name or phrase or a business method that's unique to your business, you'll want to create a competitive advantage by locking down your IP, or at least filing for it. Patenting is a cumbersome process that can take years. But filing for a provisional patent can buy you the time to build your business and get capitalized and can give investors some confidence that your business may be protected from excessive competition. If you've licensed any technology from others, you'll also want to disclose that here. If you have exclusivity in anything you've licensed, that too could be a competitive advantage.

You also want to use this section to talk about future products and services. This is a five-year plan, not just near term. You're talking about the things you want to add to your business over the next five years. Circle that back to the financial model. You may plan to introduce a new product or service in year 3, 4, or 5. You can show zeroes for that product for the first few years and then have it kick in on the financial model when you want to introduce it.

Company Analysis

When you talk about the company, you want to describe what it's all about, how it came to be, what date the company was formed or will be formed and what type of entity it is.

We talk more about the subject in *The Brass Tacks Guide to Running a Small Business*, but much depends on whether you intend to take on shareholders, how many you intend to take on, and if it's part of a larger corporate structure.

You'll also use this section to describe your office and location or locations. Show a map. Some people might not be familiar with your area, so they'll need to understand if you're close to major highways and get a sense of where you're located, especially if you're a storefront type of operation. Perhaps you want to show a larger state/regional map and then drill down to local level maps so people can see where you are in relation to the major thoroughfares in your city. If location is important, include why yours is an advantage (traffic counts, proximity to customers, etc.). If you have a location with signage, show a picture!

Discuss the current stage of your operations. Some of you are pure startups, just getting out of the gates. Others of you have existing businesses. Perhaps you're spinning something new off, you're adding something to your business, or you're just trying to raise capital. Talk about where you are currently, and what you've accomplished in the recent past.

You'll want to disclose your existing ownership structure as well as any other debts and obligations. Perhaps even your cap table if you have one ready. A lot of people fail to put this in their business plan, and it comes back to bite them later. These items are important if you are dealing with investors - you spend a lot of time and energy courting them, then months down the road, the investor finds out something that you failed to disclose to them. That won't end well.

If you have significant growth plans, you also want to account for this, both in your financial model and in this section of the plan. If your current space works for you now, what happens when you double or triple the number of employees? Is there additional space nearby you can rent? I had a medical supply company in one of the units of my initial small office building. They eventually grew into two units in our building, and then three. Finally, there just wasn't enough available space in our building for them to grow any further, and they had to find a larger space and move out.

If you are in a long-term lease of any sort, you'll want to outline those terms in the plan as well. That goes back to the comment above about obligations.

Another consideration about your company is where you're going to offer your products and services and if/how you're going to divide your territories. This won't apply to everyone, but in many cases, companies need to create local, regional, state, national, or even international plans. My consulting company, Blue Horizon Venture Consulting has helped many clients with their international expansion plans.

Finally, this section is a good place to toot your own horn over any recent or past accomplishments. Have you had previous funding? Have you invested personally in the business? How much work have you put into it (aka sweat equity)? Think of this section as being like that down payment you bring when you go to buy a house. Most lenders won't lend you 100% of the funds you need. Why should equity investors be any different? What are you bringing or have you already brought to the table?

If you've had existing products that you've had success with, talk about this. Do you have any partnerships, joint venture agreements, or supplier agreements that are important to your business? If so, talk about them here.

Operating Plan Introduction

Let's shift now into the operating plan. This is all about implementation, getting things done, and how you're going to make things happen. There are several sections to talk about. For starters, you have short-term objectives and longer-term objectives. What do operations look like on a day-to-day basis? What is your HR plan?

The idea behind the operating plan is to sort of break things down into a road map of achievement. Think of it like renovating an old building. Yeah, it's great to show a picture of what that building might look like when it's all fixed up, but to make it realistic, you need a breakdown on the major systems - electrical, plumbing, HVAC, roof, how you're going to remodel kitchens and baths, flooring, carpentry, drywall, painting, siding, landscaping, and so on. Having a project plan is mission critical.

All this is from the context of where you are now to where you want to go. If you're starting at Ground Zero, that's perfectly fine. Or, if you have a million-dollar business that you want to take to $100 million, that's great as well.

The business plan you are writing is part of your operational goals. Website/app development, product development, beta testing, launch, product/service intro, are all part of your operating plans.

The financial model can help guide the operational thinking and vice versa. Don't be afraid to toggle back and forth and make adjustments to dial in on something that is both achievable and realistic.

Operating Plan - Milestones

Whether you're creating a launch plan for a startup, or just mapping out the next year for a company that's been around for decades, having milestones is critically important. Create a short-term plan for the next year and break it down into phases - four quarters, bi-monthly, or even monthly. What key milestones will you meet and when? When can you realistically achieve each?

If you're a startup, the next quarter might be writing your business plan, submitting three loan applications, presenting to a certain number of investors, raising a certain amount of capital. The following quarter might be a beta launch with your first sales. Likewise, for existing companies, the goal might be to hire a certain number of employees, launch a new service, or hit an immediate sales growth target. This kind of goal setting and milestone creation is not only helping with investors and other interested parties, but it helps the leadership team to create "bite-sized" achievable goals, which in turn can lead to significant success. It's a pretty simple task, but so few do it. Companies are no different.

Operating Plan - Day to Day Operations

Here again is a section that business owners take for granted but that other stakeholders aren't likely to understand. What processes do you go through daily to operate your business?

Flow charts are a great way to show how things work. If you have physical products, you describe manufacturing if you're doing it yourself, or even if you're outsourcing that, how the things are getting made, how long they take to get made, who's making them, what happens when they're done, how do those products get to you or your customers?

Maybe there's transportation involved. You may be having work done off site and getting it shipped to you, perhaps manufacturing in Asia or Latin America. Things get transported to you, you then must store it somewhere, you have to maintain inventory and keep control. When your inventory gets down to a certain level, you want to reorder it.

If it's a service business, you'll describe the process flow from the beginning to end how you engage a customer.

When I work with a consulting customer at Blue Horizon Venture Consulting, my process is that I'll sit them down for an initial brainstorming session. I want a core dump of all the information they have - their files and what's in their head - we talk about everything about their business. Then I step away and focus on going through the same process we're going through here, which is building a financial model, doing all that research, starting to flesh out the plan. Lastly, I write the executive summary, then I put the investor presentation together, coaching that person on how to deliver that investor presentation.

There may be a couple of iterations of each deliverable as I work with the client to tighten everything up and get it focused. The process usually takes anywhere from 75 to 150 hours depending on the complexity of the business, the availability of information, and how involved the client is in the process. So, in my own business plan, I might create a chart for that process that describes a typical consulting engagement.

For NeurTours, I describe the customer experience when coming on a trip, from the payment process, transportation, kickoff, and what a typical day during the journey might look like, including meals, the adventure portion of the day, and the meetings/interactions with the group where we discuss what's going on with their businesses.

Another big part of your operations plan is the human resource piece. These are the staff level positions that you're going to need over time to support the growth of the company. This shouldn't be confused with the management team, which we'll discuss in a later section. For instance, if you're opening a brick-and-mortar store, then you're going to need people to stock, run the register, handle shipping & receiving, etc. If you need a sales force, then you want to discuss this and how they will get compensated (salary, commission, or both).

What will your high-level procedures be for hiring, training, and managing your staff? How will you align them with the company's goals? You don't want to recreate your employee handbook here, just the basics.

What if you're going to need any expensive equipment? What is it? How much does it cost? What does it do? What other major capital expenses might you incur at startup? Of course, this will be in your financial model, but here is where you explain what this equipment is and does and why you need it. For NeurTours, I will likely need a nice shuttle bus with comfortable seating and ample air conditioning, that can pull an equipment trailer for any domestic trips. That's a significant cost, although perhaps I won't get that equipment right away.

Will your business carry inventory? If you're filling up a retail space, obviously there's a pretty significant cost in ordering all of that inventory.

Lastly, you need to discuss quality control. How are you going to ensure that there's a certain measure of quality? What you do when you expand, when there are other people doing what you're used to doing? Obviously, you have to worry about whether they're doing it as well as you would be doing it yourself. How are you going to maintain the same level of quality that you have managed to deliver yourself? These are the questions to address here.

Operating Plan - The Org Chart

When I help clients develop an org chart, they often struggle with the exercise, usually because they are stuck in current-day thinking. If they are a startup, they scoff at the idea, because they just have one or two people, so what's the point? For existing businesses, they might even have such a chart, but it's not at all forward-looking.

It is an extremely valuable exercise. I've seen it transform a business leader's thinking. By forcing them to look five years down the road and create a full organizational chart for what their company is going to look like, if fully staffed out, they can have a very eye-opening experience, even if most of the positions say "TBD" on them. There is just some-

> There is just something about seeing that chart with dozens of positions for future team members that is very powerful for founders.

thing about seeing that chart with dozens of positions for future team members that is very powerful for founders. So, I always do it, even if I am dealing with a solopreneur enterprise, just to encourage expansive thinking. You should too.

PowerPoint has a great org chart feature with a lot of options, and of course there is other software out there capable of creating dynamic org charts as well. I like to use the version where you can include pictures of team members. It adds a personal element to the plan, and makes it seem so much more real when you see faces looking back at you.

The org chart should also align with your financial model. If you've organized your financials into different functional departments, then the org chart should show those same departments, who's in charge of each, and all the subordinates under them. Obviously, if you have a plan and expect 100 future employees, you can't show them all. If I know I'm going to need 6 admin staff, or 20 customer service reps, I'll just create one box for that position, with the corresponding number of people in parentheses.

Example Organization Chart With Pictures

Operating Plan - Timeline

A timeline is a great chart to add into your plan. These are the long-term milestones that cover your stretch goals quarter by quarter, and year by year during your five-year plan. The milestone section lays out your near-term goals. Here, you focus on your entire forecast period and perhaps even beyond.

In either case, the investments you receive are almost always going to be tied to your goals, so be very careful in how you lay them out. Make them meaningful, but achievable. Even if you aren't planning to raise capital into your business, the psychological effect of laying out your goals and achieving them can be significant and motivational for you and your team. Always remember to take time to celebrate when you achieve them.

On that investment comment, consider this - if an investor says they're going to invest $5 million into your company, many people get this idea that means they will be writing them a $5 million check or wiring $5 million into the company operating account. More often than not, that money is going to be metered out over time as you reach your milestones. You might start with $500,000 that allows you to launch and hit a customer acquisition milestone. Then, another million might get released for you to reach your next goal. This lowers risk for investors and gives them assurances that you are going to be able to execute on your plan.

5

MARKETING PLAN

Introduction to Marketing

Marketing is really the key driver behind almost every business. Without marketing, the best business idea, or the best business plan in the world, are pretty much worthless. I've read thousands of business plans over the years, and this tends to be one of the most glossed over sections in most of the poorly written plans. A lot of it is just boilerplate nonsense. Don't fall victim to this.

In truth, most operating companies probably need to put together a

> In the digital era, marketing is more complex than ever before, and you need a diverse marketing strategy with a variety of tactics, in the event one of them should suddenly become obsolete.

full-blown and separate detailed marketing plan. In the digital era, marketing is more complex than ever before, and you need a diverse marketing strategy with a variety of tactics, in the event one of them should suddenly become obsolete. Given the rate of change these days, it is almost inevitable, and you don't want to be stuck relying on only one marketing channel.

This is a section where we can tie back and get value from all that fantastic research we did earlier in the process. If you understand your market, your customers, and your competitors, then you can achieve the desired "market-message-media" match. There's nothing worse in business than just blindly throwing money at brand-style advertising with no way to measure the results from what you're doing. Brand advertising does have its time and place, but that's generally not in the early stage or high growth phases of your business.

Back in my early days, I learned an important lesson about marketing and measuring results. In the mid 1990's I was a newly minted Florida real estate agent, and I was anxious to launch my business and become instantly rich and famous. The Internet was just taking a foothold and it seemed like every day a new and shiny company was popping up that could deliver that to me. I purchased "exclusive territories" to get all the lead gen from these companies for my market area. And they delivered leads. The only problem was most of them were garbage. I either got "oh I was just looking around," or even worse, I got totally unqualified tire kickers who ran me all over town only to find out they didn't have a down payment or couldn't qualify for a mortgage. After burning tens of thousands of dollars that I could ill afford to waste, I got the message. I learned how to do better marketing myself, and to generate business effectively without losing control of my marketing budget.

Perhaps just as damaging to a business, is the old "Field of Dreams" adage, "build it, and they will come." Many a business that has taken this attitude has failed miserably, and many of them were very good companies with excellent products or services. The reality was that no one beat a path to their door, and they quickly went broke.

If you want to be effective, in good times and in bad, you need to always be marketing, and always fine-tuning your marketing to get the most out of it. And you want to have measurable marketing, so that you can gauge what's working and what's not working.

The Marketing Triangle

One of the core ideas of marketing is what's called a marketing triangle. The three points of the triangle are:

message, market and media. You really want to hit on all cylinders here because if you get one and you missed the other two, you're not going to have an effective marketing program.

The message is your unique selling proposition or USP, and it is critically important. That could be a huge driver in your business. Years ago, there were a couple of students in a college town in Michigan, and they decided that they were going to open a pizza shop near campus. One of the guys went to classes during the day and the other at night, so they could take turns running the restaurant.

These guys came up with the idea of delivering pizza to hungry college students late at night. The partners argued about it and one of them said he didn't want to do delivery and he left. The other guy came up with a slogan, and you've probably heard it before, but it goes a little something like "hot fresh pizza delivered in 30 minutes or less." And eventually this small college town restaurant grew into Domino's Pizza, based on that unique selling proposition.

It's so important to get that message out there, a message that strikes a chord with people, that makes sense to them, and that they connect with. But you still have to hit the other legs of this triangle. You have to hit the right market. Marketing to a 50-year-old with young kids who are in bed at 8pm, probably wasn't the right market. But college students up late studying, or participating in other activities that make them hungry, is a pretty good market match.

And finally, the last leg of this triangle is the media that you use, and the worst number in business is one. Using only one media is almost always a mistake. It makes perfect sense to use multiple forms of media because a lot of people take in information in different channels. Some people watch TV, some people read the paper. Some people listen to the radio and some people are online. So, you want to make sure that you have a multi-channel multimedia approach and that you're out there hitting your target market in different ways so that they have the opportunity to capture your message and act on it.

That's the core of what marketing is all about it, and that's what gets results. You want to address it in your business plan by letting investors know that you have thought these things out and you've done your research, and that you're coming up with a coherent marketing strategy that's going to reach your intended audience.

Message

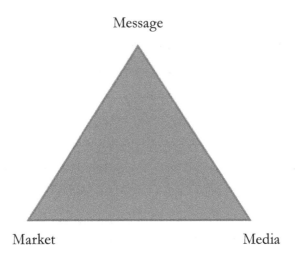

Market   Media

The Four P's of Marketing

I should pause here to make a comment about brand versus direct response marketing. There is certainly a time
and a place for both. Traditionally, what has been taught in
colleges and universities has been brand marketing, which
can generally be a significant waste of money, particularly
for startups and early-stage ventures.

Frankly, there is something to be learned from both
camps, but as a general rule of thumb, stick to direct response
marketing until you are generating at least $1 million in
annual revenues, then you can worry about branded marketing and expanding your reach. There's a reason why the
failure rate of early-stage companies is so high, and besides

a lack of capital, a failure to embrace direct response or "guerilla" marketing tends to be a close second. Restaurants tend to have a "build it and they will come" attitude, which is why there is so much failure in the industry.

What should high growth ventures concern themselves about traditional brand marketing concepts? Let's discuss the four P's of marketing. I was taught this in undergraduate school and when I got my MBA. It certainly is worth understanding, and it is worth mentioning in the context of your business plan narrative.

First is **P**roducts, and we've already crafted an extensive product section. But your message needs to convey what it is you're selling and how it benefits your customers, and that's really what it's all about. The benefit to your customers is the critical piece. What is the value proposition of your products or services for your customers? You need to answer this question in your plan.

Price is a very complex subject. What value does your price convey relative to what they could get from competitors? And what's the value you're giving in exchange for that price? You really don't want to compete on price. You can charge a lot more than your competitors if you provide your customers with value and they see the value that you're giving. Often, that's a matter of putting in the effort to provide that extra service or group of service benefits or bonuses that makes customers feel like they're getting value. There are a lot of books out there on pricing strategy, worth checking into before you set yours.

Place - where your products can be purchased, be it in a brick and mortar store or selling online. Is there anything special about where you're located or about your company? That's an extra benefit or value to customers. I once had a client in the art supply business. Art supplies in and of themselves aren't especially exciting - you'll find the same things, more or less, in pretty much any art supply store. What she did to differentiate herself on place was to create a café environment with food, coffee/tea and an outdoor space where artists could congregate, relax, or actually draw/paint in the courtyard. While Amazon and other online retailers really have had a huge impact on this business segment, she managed to offer customers a place that they could not.

Promotion, the final P, is how you go about reaching your customers. What channels will you use to make customers aware of your business? PR, direct mail, radio, print, social media, email, sales, etc. Certainly, the digital era has turned promotion on its head, and you should definitely cover the bases if you're going to be marketing online. That said, it's important to have a marketing mix and to utilize more than one channel, preferably a mix of online and offline tactics, but particularly online, where your business could easily come to a screeching halt if just one company like Facebook arbitrarily decides to change the way it manages its online advertising platform, as it has done a number of times in the past.

The Five F's of Customer Needs

It is also important to show how your product meets a customer's basic needs. As a general rule, most things being sold fit into one of three categories: health, wealth, and relationships. There are five customer needs that you should consider in light of these categories and what customers seek:

Function - Does your product serve a certain purpose? What is the function?

Finances - What's the price advantage or savings over alternate choices?

Freedom - Does this purchase of your products save your customers time and effort in some way?

Feelings - Does your product or service enhance a customer's self-image? Does it provide a sense of security? Or does it provide some sort of pleasure or some other kind of intangible benefit? Most buying is done based on emotion and rationalized after the fact.

Future - What benefits will customers gain in the future? Time saved, effort saved, money gained, etc. What will their future state look like?

Online Marketing

Online marketing has definitely exploded in the last 20 years. While it certainly makes a lot of sense to learn as much as possible about online marketing, it's still worth noting that traditional forms of marketing are still very effective, and in fact, can be more effective as less people utilize them. Regardless, be careful about putting all your online eggs into one basket. There are countless horror stories of people being cut off by Google or Facebook, for various infractions. All of a sudden, they just can't advertise anymore. If you are in that situation and your business is completely reliant on one source, you're in a lot of trouble.

SEO/SEM - Search engine optimization and search engine marketing are really all about providing quality content and information, not on trying to shortcut the system, which will eventually catch up to you. If you make a continuous effort to publish content, you can start to develop organic traffic.

Online Advertising or Pay Per Click (PPC) - This is probably the fastest way to generate online business. It's also one of the most expensive, unfortunately, and this is an area where you can waste a lot of money if you don't know what you're doing, so it pays to learn this before you throw thousands of dollars away trying to learn things the hard way. Hiring an expert can save you a fair bit of money. You'll want to discuss how you intend to drive traffic through paid advertising, and on what sites you will advertise. Have a specific budget in mind.

Social Media Marketing - This is a massive and growing business and another potential black hole into which you might throw money if you're not careful. Many people think of social media as a silly waste of time, and there's some truth to that in that these platforms are designed to be "sticky" or to get people addicted to using them. The amount of time people spend on Facebook and Instagram is appalling. But underlying that, there's a very, very powerful business engine that's driving tons of traffic.

Website - This is your online hub, and you want to build and manage your website in a way that that's very effective and you want to show this in your business plan. You may want to add a few screenshots of your website, and perhaps a schematic about your process flow. How you capture leads, what you do with a lead once you get it, and what CRM or other tools underlie your site? Creating a good website that not only showcases your business but attracts customers, offering them something in exchange for "opting in" with their information, starting with an email address is important. Building a list of potential customers who opt in is always the starting point online. I never cease to be amazed by people who invest huge sums into creating a website, which does nothing to engage potential customers other than perhaps giving them a phone number to call.

Does your website have a shopping cart? If you are allowing people to place orders online, there's a couple of things underlying that. You need a merchant account to accept credit card payments, or you could just accept PayPal payments. Explain the systems and software you will use. Many of these tools can take the place of full-time employees in your business and can show stakeholders that you are using technology wisely.

At the end of the day, your online presence is all about creating traffic, capturing leads, and then marketing to those leads when you get them in a way that optimizes your revenue while creating the highest possible returns on your investments. It's a beautiful thing to be generating business 24-7-365 and to go to sleep and wake up in the morning and have leads and business coming in.

Public Relations

Depending on the nature of your business, you may be able to generate some free publicity for your business by engaging newspaper writers, TV /radio reporters, magazine writers, or bloggers to run stories about you or your business. Get a mention from the right outlet and sales can go through the roof. That is what PR can do for you, depending on your industry and your market.

You'd be surprised how much writers and TV/ radio reporters are out there trying to find a good story, and they're actually in some cases fairly desperate to find stories. There's a website called HARO (help a reporter out) that lists the types of people reporters are looking to interview for certain topics. If your business fits the bill, it may be a good chance to get some recognition.

Get to know some of the members of the press in your local area, especially if you're a local brick and mortar store. And every time you get featured anyway, you will always and forever be able to use the "as seen on/in" tool in your other forms of marketing, if you do what's called "spider-webbing," which is essentially keeping a piece of content alive and expanding its use to other pieces of content.

I do want to point out here that there is a large distinction between earned media and paid media. You can just as easily pay your way into getting media appearances and mentions as you can getting them for free.

You might want to think about hiring a PR firm to manage this work for you. There are some big time New York Fifth Avenue PR firms that are extremely expensive and can get you on shows like The Today Show and other major programs. But there are other, less expensive shops out there with more moderate goals like the local newspapers and the business journals in your area.

You can also do some of the legwork yourself, such as writing your own press releases, and you never know where it may lead. Somebody could see something you're doing, and that could lead to something else.

Back in 2011, I decided to go on an RV road trip with my dog, driving around the country writing business plans for companies that were trying to get established in the wake of the Great Mortgage Meltdown recession. I didn't really intend for anything to go beyond that, but I actually got contacted by someone interested in doing reality television based on a similar concept. Once you get your name out there, things can snowball and unexpected things can happen that can be really beneficial for you and your company.

Traditional Advertising

There is a saying in the real estate investment world, and it essentially says when the media is talking about how great real estate is going, it's time to sell. And when they are talking about how down in the dumps it is, it's time to buy. In other words, sometimes going against the grain of what everyone else is doing can be extremely beneficial.

So, it seems that the world is enamored and engrossed in online advertising, and they tend to forget about all of the "old-fashioned" ways to get noticed. So much so, in fact, that the pricing for traditional forms of media has become a little more favorable as traditional media is forced to compete with digital.

I will say it again for emphasis that a multimedia, multi-channel approach is what most businesses should have. Just like you should not invest your entire life savings into one stock investment, so too should you diversify your marketing.

Consider television ads. Cable ads are a lot cheaper than you might think they are, so it is worth contacting your local provider to find out what their ad rates are. You can often find an excellent demographic match, if not a topical match for your product or service. Say you

> A multimedia, multi-channel approach is what most businesses should have. Just like you should not invest your entire life savings into one stock investment, so too should you diversify your marketing.

had a bridal shop business in your local market area. Then advertising on a show like *Bridezillas* or something similar might provide a good match. Or say you had a product or service that caters to seniors, then you might find that a cable station that shows reruns of "Matlock" or "I Love Lucy" or other such nostalgic shows which will give you good exposure to your demographic target.

Radio is the most captive audience you can find, and the best hours (and most expensive) are generally during the morning and evening commutes, aka "drive time." Most people are generally in their cars when they listen to radio, so they're not going anywhere. If you find a good match with your audience (like a fitness product or gym during a sports talk program), you will not only get good exposure to your target audience, but repeat exposure as well, which can be particularly valuable.

Radio is unique, too, because it involves "theater of the mind," where people can use their imaginations when they listen to you. This is a unique opportunity to "get inside their heads." You can also make it sound like you are talking directly to them, which can be powerful. Again, radio is not necessarily as expensive as many people think. Also, there are media aggregators who go out and buy up time on radio stations in bulk, then resell it in packages. You can go through an aggregator and get a lot of airtime inexpensively. Radio can be an excellent option, especially if you've got a local focus and a radio show where the demographics line up with your ideal customers.

Magazines can be a great place to advertise and are often focused on very specific topics. You might be surprised how many different types of magazines you've never heard of that line up with your industry. There are probably a few in everyone's industry, so right off the bat, they are great targets. You may also have different products that are better fits for specific magazines where you can advertise into exact niches.

Newspapers are sort of a dying breed of advertising. If you still subscribe to a newspaper and get it delivered, you know they are much, much thinner than they used to be. The industry has gone into a death spiral, which starts when they lose advertising and readership to the Internet. In response, they raise their advertising and subscription rates, and they drive more business away.

On the flip side, however, it is now easier than ever to stand out in a newspaper. They have far fewer pages and a lot less advertising, so your chances of getting noticed are quite a bit higher. I ran a marketing group in Jacksonville, Florida for several years, and one of our regular members drove a large percentage of his business that targeted men, by advertising in the sports section of the local newspaper.

You can negotiate terms with the papers, especially if you intend to do long term advertising. You can also do flyer inserts in the newspaper that allows you to target down to specific zip codes where they distribute the paper. This can cost less than direct mail to deliver the same content (no envelope, no stamp needed).

While the future of the post office is somewhat cloudy, I cannot imagine that it won't exist in some way, shape, or form indefinitely. So much communication has moved online. If you have lived for any length of time, you know that we used to get a lot more mail than we do these days. When's the last time you got a hand-written letter from someone?

Direct mail is a chance to stand out if you do something that's unique and interesting and grabs people's attention. You can get a super-targeted list from providers like InfoUSA and know you are mailing only to a specific list. It's amazing how they can slice and dice information.

Think about all the different surveys you've done and how much information they really get from you - age, your income, where you live, your ZIP code, whether you have kids, interests, hobbies, etc. This ability to drill down to a list of your avatar customers is powerful.

At one point in my career, I was considering running an entrepreneurial camp for kids. It was easy to get a list of people with kids in a certain age range, with a higher household income, who lived within a fairly short drive of where I wanted to hold the camp. If you deliver that message at the right time of year when families are trying to make their summer plans, it would be super effective. And repetition helps as well. Better to mail to a targeted list half a dozen times than to shotgun your message to a much larger audience, most of whom won't have any interest.

> Whatever marketing channels you use, be sure you set them up in a way where you can measure results.

There are a few other marketing tactics worth mentioning: billboards, yellow pages, special events, and movie theater advertising come to mind. Whatever marketing channels you use, be sure you set them up in a way where you can measure results. For instance, say you used a billboard. Use a unique URL or phone number, and then you'll be able to attribute your inbound traffic to that specific advertising. It's amazingly cheap to set up URLs and phone numbers that get forwarded into your main website or your main phone line. Then at least you'll know where your traffic is coming from.

Trade Shows & Associations

Not only can associations and trade shows be a great source of education for you in your industry, they can provide countless leads and/or opportunities to create joint ventures with other business owners who may have complimentary businesses. Almost every industry has an association you can join, and if yours doesn't, it may be an opportunity for you to create one! After all, every association had to get started by someone.

Another thing to keep in mind is that associations generally have access to lists or directories, although you should be careful not to break any association rules on soliciting other members.

Next to paid online advertising, trade shows can be one of the quickest ways that to generate sales and ramp up your business.

With trade shows, you really have two options - you can just attend and do as much networking as possible during the event (and often this is a good way to start out, to make sure the show is a good fit), or you can pay to be a sponsor or pay for a booth at the show where you can display your company and try to draw in potential customers.

I have to admit that early in my career, I was a horrible networker. Being somewhat of an introvert, I found it difficult to talk to people all day, and I dreaded the process. Then I partnered up on a business venture with someone from New York who was tremendous at this, and I went to several shows with him and watched how he operated. He would come out of an event with a massive pile of business cards, and would know everything about just about everyone there, even guys like me, who might rather be watching a football game back in my room than gladhanding until 1am like he did. What I learned, however, was that there is value in meeting people in person, shaking their hands, looking them in the eye, getting to know them, and maybe even having a meal, a beer, or a coffee with them.

So over time, I have forced myself to do a better job at this, and now I've gotten to the point where I actually enjoy it in limited doses.

Doing your research on local, regional, national, or even international trade shows is a good idea. Even if you don't plan to attend them all, showcasing a list in your business plans shows that you know what's going on in your industry and that you plan to be a big part of it.

Marketing ROI

Measuring your marketing return on investment (MROI), is absolutely critical. And there are a few key marketing metrics that you will want to include in your business plan as well.

Why the fuss over MROI? If you don't measure it, it's just like rolling the dice. You won't know what's effective and what's not. Without accurate measurement of marketing spend results, you can end up repeating your mistakes and throwing away tons of money.

Thanks to the technological age, there are a lot of tools that can help you track your marketing effectiveness. Software allows you to do what's called "split testing," where you test two different web pages or two different emails or different colors, and it's amazing what you can find out. There have been split tests where one color pulled like 40% more traffic than another color did, just by changing the background color. By constantly testing against and improving your "control" you can optimize your marketing and MROI. And when something works, and you can measure it, you can then do more of that same style of marketing, or invest more money into a campaign, because you know it's delivering positive results for your company.

The key metrics you want to include in your business plan include your acquisition costs, or how much money you have to spend for each new customer you bring on board, and also, lifetime customer value, or how much that customer will spend for as long as they are your customer. If you don't at least have an estimate of these numbers, you're doing yourself and your business a big disservice, and you'll likely turn off investors who are attuned to these metrics.

For acquisition costs, it's pretty easy to measure. You expect to add 1,000 customers in your first year, and you are going to spend $500,000 on marketing. Your acquisition cost is then $500 per customer. You can also add a great level of detail to this in terms of leads (people who opt for something in exchange for getting marketing from you) versus customers. After all, once someone becomes a lead, you can market to them until they become a customer, opt out, or die. You may also have metrics like "cost per action," "cost per conversion," or other items on your marketing/MROI dashboard.

LCV is a metric that is often overlooked, but it is critically important. Do your customers come in once, buy something, and then they are done, never to be heard from again? Do they buy every 5 years? Are they on a monthly subscription where they stick around for an average of five years? Answers to these types of questions can help you determine the lifetime customer value. Consider, for example, the above case where we spent $500,000 to acquire 1,000 customers. Each customer pays $25/month for our software, and they stick around for an average of four years. So, we know that we're bringing in $1,200 in revenue from each customer over their average LCV. Spending $500 to make $1,200 may be reasonable, depending on the other costs of your business. Often, finding ways to increase the LCV of your existing customer base can be one of the most profitable activities you can undertake.

6

MANAGEMENT

Management Team

Every business plan needs a management team, whether you're a solopreneur with advisors or a large organization. One of the first things investors look at when evaluating a plan is who is involved in it. If your team doesn't pass the sniff test, a lot of times your plan will wind up in the round file (aka the garbage can). Many investors are really busy, and they just don't have the time to look through every deal, so they often take shortcuts, and this is one of them. You definitely want to have a strong management team section. And it's possible, even if you are a lone first-time owner. It's always possible to build the team around you. And even if you don't have your entire team in place, you can create the positions you will eventually want to have filled. Who knows, the person reading the plan may know just the right person! You'll want to describe each person's function, the type of background needed, etc.

Your background and experience are critically important as well. A lot of people don't like writing about themselves, but you really need to let people know who you are, your experience, and your passion for your venture. It will show in your bio (or not). If you have a track record in other ventures, lay it out here for people to see. Past experience is valuable.

If you don't have a lot of experience, there are certainly ways to build a team around you, which we'll talk about in the next section.

You can also discuss here how you're going to incentivize your employees, including stock options, bonuses, and benefits.

Advisors & Directors

Every business has advisors, and this is where you want to showcase them, especially if you don't have a large staff at present. Accountants, attorneys, business consultants, web designers, and others can be considered part of your team. I am often asked to be included as an advisor in my clients' plans, and my background can add a decent amount of credibility to the team. Sometimes, our team at Blue Horizon Venture Consulting will even take on an interim executive role, like CEO, COO, or CFO, all things we have done in the past. Hiring someone on an interim/ fractional basis can be a fantastic way to build your team without a major salary outlay or long-term commitment.

That said, you always want to ask someone's permission before you include them in your plan. Generally, it's free advertising for service providers, so they are more than likely to say yes, especially if you ask nicely.

Director is a more formal role within the company, and it's something a lot of early-stage ventures neglect. In fact, there is quite a bit of neglect when it comes to the formalities of running a business that many people blow off, and wish they hadn't further down the road. Creating a board of directors, holding meetings, setting up an accounting system, creating an operating agreement, and creating employment contracts are all good examples of this. Founders get too caught up in their development or their day-to-day operations, or they think they are too small for all of that business formality, and then a year or so down the road, they regret not having laid this groundwork and often have to dig out of a huge mess in order to set things right. Take a little time and set things up properly from the outset.

The value in having a Board of Directors from the outset is they can offer you a lot of advice, industry connections, and experience that you might not otherwise have. Think about people you know in your industry or in your field and ask them to be members of your board. It's not a huge commitment from them.

You can sometimes offer them some money or you could give them stock options, maybe even products from your company. Very often the people you ask will be flattered. More often than not, people really do want to help you, and people generally love the underdog person starting a business. And consider this, there are a lot of retired executives out there who might otherwise be itching for an opportunity to somehow "stay in the game" while still enjoying their retirement. A board seat could do just that for them. Your board can add a great deal of credibility to your business plan as well as to your business.

The Board of Directors can have a lot of power to make strategic decisions. You can outline all of that in your operating agreement. You can create just an advisory board or you can build a real board of directors that has the power to hire and fire a CEO. You clearly want to articulate how the Board will operate and what's expected of members.

Investors will often want a seat on your board. You generally want to be the chairman. They're investing in your business and they're likely going to want to have some sort of say in how things are run, and they want to make sure that you're doing things the right way.

With the entire management section, don't just regurgitate resumes. Tell very brief and interesting stories about each person on the team, what they've accomplished in their life, and perhaps write a bit about their pertinent work experience. Just a few sentences to a few paragraphs should suffice. You don't want to list every job someone's had in their entire career - just hit the high points of the most relevant positions.

One thing you want to ensure is that the information in your management section agrees with your organizational chart and that both of those agree with the numbers in your financial model. This is a mistake I've seen happen fairly often when the sections get written at different times.

7

LOGO CREATION

Image is everything. The picture you use to tell the world what your business is all about is one of the first things people see when they are introduced to your company. What does it say about you and your business? Is your company fun and energetic? Serious and trustworthy? You only get one chance to make a first impression, and often your logo is it.

That being the case, isn't it worth a little time and effort to put your best foot forward?

There are a number of ways to go about creating a logo. If you're an expert graphic designer, then you can probably create your own. But there are a ton of online services these days where you can have logos created, often very inexpensively. Fiverr is a good example of a cheap source for logos.

My personal favorite is a site called Hatchwise, which is a site where you can hold a contest for a logo design, and you only have to pay the winner. You advise them of the name of your company, and the colors and features you want to see, and you set a prize amount for the winner, generally a few hundred dollars. From this, you will likely get anywhere from a dozen to a hundred different entries. This allows you to browse through and select the one you like the best.

Years ago, I was working on a carbon nanotube startup out of Florida State University. We were looking for a logo for our new company so I decided to take the ten logos I liked best from the Hatchwise contest I was running and ask the stakeholders in the company to vote on which one they liked best. I tallied up the results and picked the winner based on everyone's input. Not only did we come up with a super cool logo, but everyone felt they had participated in the process to boot!

A few things to think about as it relates to what you want. Will you include text in the logo, like the name of the company or a slogan? Or do you just want a symbol?

You also want something that will stand out whether printed in black and white or in color. If your logo totally washes out in black and white, you will likely want to revise it.

Color selection can also be very important. Colors tend to convey certain ideas subliminally to people, so do some research into what colors might best convey the image you're going for.

You can also poll your existing customers, clients, or prospects to get their input into your logo. This can be a great way to engage them and build rapport without asking them to buy something. Surveymonkey.com and other survey tools are a great way to go about soliciting feedback like this from people on your lists.

8

FINANCIAL PLAN

Financial Plan Intro

As we enter the latter sections of the plan, we're wrapping a bow around the work we've already done to this point. We've gone through the marketing plan and the operations plan. We've looked at the product section. We've done all the market research on customers, competitors, the market, and the industry.

But recall we started the whole process by setting up the framework of our financial model. Having gone through this entire process, you should now be able to start tweaking those numbers based on the data that you're mining about your market, the size of the market, and about how many potential customers exist, so that you can come up with a more refined forecast.

A good model is set up so that it is super easy to change assumptions and the entire financial model will automatically update.

Pulling graphics and nicely formatted tables from your financial forecast can really enhance your business plan as well. You can certainly attach all the financial detail in an appendix, but you only want to present relevant high-level data in your plan.

If you're using your business plan to raise capital, you want your financial section to be as bulletproof as possible. More often than not, the questions investors ask are meant to poke holes in your plan and

Think of it like rowing your boat across a pond. The investors are trying to shoot holes in your boat with their questions to see if you can get to the other side.

challenge your assumptions. So, the more defensible your assumptions, the better chance you have of success. Think of it like rowing your boat across a pond. The investors are trying to shoot holes in your boat with their questions to see if you can get to the other side, or if your boat will sink if they shoot too many holes in it. Yes, this is a somewhat adversarial idea, and you certainly don't want to be defensive in a meeting with investors. You simply want to be prepared with answers so that you safely cross that pond and survive their questioning intact. Often, you can get some good ideas from their feedback. Being gracious enough to take it in stride versus getting defensive is always a good way to go. You can improve and tweak your plan after every interaction, so even if you don't succeed with a given investor, you've gotten something useful out of the meeting.

In the financial section of the plan, you want to summarize your model in a narrative form. You want to tell the story about what's going to happen your first five years in business. You want to explain how you arrived at your assumptions based on all the research you did, not just random guesses or pie in the sky numbers. Having a justification for the numbers in your plan can make a world of difference.

Certainly, keeping your audience in mind in this section is important. You may want to talk a little differently to investors than you might to your internal team or to a potential JV partner.

If you're raising capital, you can't forget to ask for it. Tell readers how much capital you need, and how you intend to employ it. Don't be too rigid in setting a valuation or terms. Often, it's better to leave this open to negotiation. Bear in mind, too, that you may be talking to both equity investors and debt lenders.

If your plan succeeds in getting peoples' interest and getting them to the negotiating table, you're 95% of the way there.

Explaining Your Assumptions

You want to use a little of your business plan real estate to explain how you arrived at the core assumptions for your model.

How did you arrive at the volume of business that you projected in that financial model? You want to be realistic in your sales projections, but not overly conservative such that you sell yourself short, either. How will your sales volumes ramp up over time? You can either attack this issue from the perspective of the market and capturing a certain percentage of the market, or you could look at it from an internal perspective and state that you have a certain amount of capacity that you expect to be used. Let's say with NeurTours, I find that my avatar market is business owners who subscribe to National Geographic Traveler magazine. Suppose I find that 100,000 people fit this category. That's my target market. Let's say I engage 1,000 people from my marketing in the first year, and that number increases by 1000 each year, such that I engage 5,000 people by the fifth year. From those people who opt in to my marketing, a certain percentage come on trips, and of those, perhaps half become repeat customers who return every year. You may be able to find information on competitors that gives you a good baseline.

How did you set your pricing? Hopefully it's set based on the value received by customers and not via some arbitrary cost-plus number or based on what others are charging in the market. Regardless, you'll want to explain why you have higher or lower prices. This points to the notion of differentiation - what makes your company unique and a better choice for your customers?

Expense assumptions are important as well. While you may not want to put too much detail in about them, understanding some of your largest costs are important. Cost of Goods Sold (COGS) is a good one to explain in this section. What major capital expenditures will you have to make now and in the future? What will your personnel and sales team costs look like? Do you have to contend with shipping, logistics, and storage costs? If you're a tech company, what will you have to pay for bandwidth and storage?

Marketing assumptions are also important, and this ties back to your volume assumptions. If you understand what it costs to acquire each customer, and the lifetime value of each customer, those assumptions will drive a lot of your financials. The detail in the model will speak for itself, but a summary of your expected marketing expenses and major categories of expense are helpful.

General and administrative costs are important to note as well. This ties back to what we talked about in the operations section. What is your real estate plan - rent versus purchase? What other major expenses will you have? Travel, telephone, utilities, insurance?

Financials- HR

Human resource costs, whether employees or contractors, is often one of the largest expenses of many companies. How did you arrive at your salary or wage numbers? Are they competitive? What are your competitors paying their employees?

If your goal is to attract and retain the best in your industry, you're going to pay a little bit more.

You also want to make sure there is logic in your total headcount numbers and the size of your business as it grows over time. If your business is somewhat labor intensive, it's important to be realistic here.

You'll also want to talk about your benefits plan, if you will offer stock options, what you're going to do to attract and retain your key employees. Perhaps you'll offer more in the way of incentives and less in salary in the early stages in order to preserve capital. Here is where you'll want to explain that.

Lastly, you'll want to explain what functions you intend to outsource and when/if you plan to bring them in house at some point. As mentioned previously, Blue Horizon Venture Consulting will often step into an interim role, let's say as a fractional CFO. We help a client set up their books, get funding, manage payroll/benefits, and do monthly/quarterly/annual reporting and tax work. We might do this for the first two years a company is in operations, at which point they have grown large enough that they can hire their own controller or CFO to manage those items. The business plan would show outsourced costs for this work for two years and then an additional salaried position starting in year three.

The Financial Forecast

You will want to show your high level five-year forecast summary in this section. This will show the revenues, high level expenses and net income over the first five years of the business. This gives readers a pretty comprehensive picture on what you expect to happen in the business over this time period, and it conveys a lot of information in a small space.

You'll want to explain what is happening, particularly if you show losses or rapidly changing numbers in your forecast. Beware of showing the "hockey stick" forecast, where you show low numbers or losses in the early stage and then a sudden and magic rise from there. At the very least, have a reasonable explanation if you show this.

The model should also show the point at which your business breaks even, and you might want to provide an even more exact date in this section. For example, if your summary model shows positive income in year two, you should state that you will break even in month 15, 20, or whatever the actual case may be.

If there is anything else that sticks out, be prepared to explain why in this section. Perhaps you are purchasing more equipment in year three where you might show a loss for that year, then significantly increased revenues in years four and five. Or you might add a new product or products in a certain year, or build an internal sales force, which in turn impacts the numbers. The trick is to answer the inevitable questions that will spring up in the reader's mind before they can even ask them.

In essence, you are telling the story of how you'll make money, using your forecast model as the backdrop.

Financing & Exit Strategy

This is an absolutely critical section in a business plan, that amazingly, some people forget to include! It's really the culmination of all of the work you've done to put it together, as it states what you need to drive the business forward. If you are using the plan to raise capital, it explains how much you need, and what you intend to use it for. Further, it explains how you're going to repay that capital - be it income from operations, another round of financing in the future, joint venture, or a merger/acquisition.

Again, this should not be some pie in the sky number, but a well-reasoned and clearly justified ask, based on the numbers in the plan you have laid out. Explain if you are using the money to hire key personnel, purchase specific equipment, purchasing inventory/raw materials, or setting up a marketing campaign, or some combination thereof. Ideally, you can show how the investment will give you enough time (or "runway") to make the business profitable. Running out of capital is one of the leading causes of failure, and as counterintuitive as it sounds, even companies that are seeing a massive amount of success can run into cash flow problems.

There is an old adage in business that it generally takes twice as long and three times as much capital as expected to make a business work. You should always build some sort of cushion into your forecasting and capital raising to give you and your stakeholders a little extra comfort. You may discover another opportunity you want to explore. Or you may incur some expenses you didn't anticipate. Either way, having some extra resources for such contingencies is important.

That said, if you've gone through this entire process, and created a well-articulated plan, you are far less likely to be caught by surprise by the unanticipated.

When you discuss exit strategies for the business, you really want to think about your business from the perspective of the investor. Their number one thought is typically - how am I going to get that money back? Followed closely thereafter by - what are my returns going to be? Then - how long is it going to take?

You want investors to feel confident in your abilities and that you are mitigating their risks to the greatest extent possible. Most investors realize the risks involved with early-stage companies. But they also like the upside, and the potential for a "home run" type of return, which can be anywhere from five times to ten times (5x-10x) on their investment. The general rule is that investors understand that not all of their investments will succeed, so they are looking for some of them to create significant returns to make up for the investments that fail.

Not all investors think this way, however. If you have friends and family involved or less seasoned investors, they may be fine with an 8-10% return on their investment. After all it beats the near zero returns on funds parked in a bank or a low-yield mutual fund!

Ideally, you can list a number of exit options for investors. An IPO is not a realistic option for most small businesses, although it does represent a crowning achievement for many early-stage companies who make it that far. There are certainly other options, like reverse mergers into a public shell company, mergers with larger private companies, joint ventures, additional financing, and payments from existing cash flows that can also pay back investors.

Debt financing is also an option that avoids dealing with equity investors, as the terms of repayment are clearly defined. The downside to debt is that it hurts your early cash flows as you are forced to make periodic payments on it. Equity capital is generally far more patient, but it can be significantly more expensive in the long run. Sometimes, using a balance of debt and equity capital is a smart way to go.

Lastly, you do want to think about your own ultimate goals for the business. Do you plan to run it for your entire career? Pass it on to your children? Or perhaps do you want to grow it for a few years, then sell it off and move on to your next venture (or adventure)? Beginning with the end in mind is always a wise idea, so that you can work backward in your planning and execution to achieve that ultimate vision. I never cease to be amazed by how many people start a business, never having thought about how they want to exit it. Do yourself a favor, and think about that before you ever start writing your business plan. It can be a helpful frame of reference for how you construct your plan.

One final note is to make sure that you clearly articulate how much of your own capital has been invested in the business to date. Having significant "skin in the game" is important to stakeholders for a number of reasons, chief among them is that you are completely invested in your idea and have put your own valuable resources at risk. I sometimes have to cajole this information out of my clients because they have kept poor records and they really have no idea how much of their own money they have sunk into their projects. It can be eye-opening if a client has been working on their business for years.

9

RISKS & MITIGATING FACTORS

Whether your plan is intended for equity investors, debt lenders, or internal stakeholders, many people will view your company through the lens of risk. It's inherent in pretty much any type of business, so thinking through all of the potential risks of your business and discussing your strategy for mitigating those risks, can be a powerful addition to your business plan. It can also serve as a CYA with anyone you present to, should one of those risks crop up over time.

There are normal risks that likely affect every business. Discuss those. Then, there are probably a few risks specific to your industry, or perhaps to your location. Be open and forthcoming about these risks. Preemptively addressing these items is far better than having to defend them in person in a meeting with investors and stumbling through an answer.

If you're a startup, there will be some risks specific to launch. Do you have intellectual property? Are there barriers to entry or could someone easily copy your model and beat you at your own game? Are you relying on first mover advantage? How will you market to customers and will they be interested in what you offer? Are there any technology risks (i.e., being reliant on Google or Facebook who can shut you down without notice)?

It your data safe and protected, perhaps backed up on the cloud? Is your equipment reliable? Your website? How will you prevent hacking?

We have a list of common risks that you can download if you visit www.brasstacksbooks.com/WWBP.

There are, of course marketing risks, so you can reiterate how you are going to reach customers and sustain your business over the long haul.

You also have operational risks. How are your sales fulfilled? If you have a physical product, what's the supply chain and what happens to your business if your key supplier gets disrupted in some way? Maybe their warehouse catches on fire. Do you have redundant sources of supply? Same thing on the distribution side. If you are reliant on retail sales partners, what happens if your main channel suddenly files for bankruptcy or shutters all of its stores, something that has sadly become common in recent times. What sort of service partners do you rely on? Subcontractors? One person not performing can throw off an entire team or process.

There are legal risks. What happens if a law or regulation in your industry is changed? Some industries have a lot of regulation. Health care is a good example where new laws turned the health insurance market on its head.

And of course, there are macroeconomic risks, the Black Swan events of history such as 9/11, the mortgage meltdown, and the Covid-19 pandemic. Or hurricanes and fires. Does your company have contingency plans for these types of events? If not, you should, and you should also be prepared to answer questions about how you might survive such incidents or if you are insured against them.

Economic risks and demographic shifts can also affect a business. Can your business survive a recession or is your business predicated on a healthy economy? Are people moving to your market area or away from it? This ties back to the demographic research you did earlier, where (hopefully) you are showing strong growth trends that will support your business.

10

THE EXECUTIVE SUMMARY

Executive Summary Introduction

Congratulations if you've made it this far and have done all the work to get your business plan completed. Take a break, and step away, as this next section is absolutely the most important section you will write. You want to be on your A game when you write it. The executive summary is the window to your business plan. This is what people are going to read first. This is your first chance to make a good impression in writing.

Think about this from the perspective of someone with 100 business plans on their desk. They have to sift through them and pick out the top ten plans. The problem is, they only have a few hours to do so. No way will they have the time to read 100 business plans in their entirety.

So what do they do? They read the executive summaries to quickly scan through the pile to get down to the plans they actually want to invest time in reading. The ones that are unclear or overly verbose, quickly get tossed in the trash. The goal of your executive summary is to get them reading more. You want to hook them with an intriguing first line, and high level, interesting details that will make them want to dig in for more information.

What you're trying to do in your executive summary is to condense the major sections of your plan down into a few short paragraphs. Yes, you will repeat statements made in the plan, and that's OK. Your executive summary should be able to stand alone as its own document in addition to being the lead of your full business plan.

This section should be two to three hard-hitting pages and no more. I see a lot of people try to force too much detail into the executive summary, essentially rewriting entire sections. That's a common mistake. You goal is not to give readers all of the information about your business. Your goal is to make them curious and interested enough to keep reading.

> Your goal is to make them curious and interested enough to keep reading.

Executive Summary - The Overview

The overview is the first paragraph of your plan. Spending some time on crafting your opening sentence is a worthwhile exercise. There's an old story about Ernest Hemingway entering a shortest novel contest and coming up with "For sale: baby shoes, never worn." This triggers an avalanche of questions about what happened and immediately makes the reader want to learn more about the situation.

A good exercise is to write a dozen opening lines, and then narrow it down to your three favorites. Then refine those, and perhaps solicit some feedback from others to see what they think and if the sentence makes them curious about your business. Most people won't do this. Most people won't have a good opening line.

Once you have that key opening sentence, you want to add a couple more descriptive sentences that support it and that kind of help round out the description of what your business is all about. To give you an example, here's my NeurTours opening line, and it's just to give you a sense of what I'm trying to convey.

"NeurTours is an exciting business-building adventure travel company which unplugs entrepreneurs from their day-to-day distracted worlds, immerses them in challenging physical experiences, while using the power of collective thinking to help inspire game-changing creative breakthroughs."

This sentence describes what we do to a T, but it also leaves a reader wondering how we do it, what kind of trips we go on, and so on. You'll want to add a few more sentences to solidify your description, particularly if you have a complex business model, but again, avoid the urge to overexplain here.

Executive Summary - Problem and Opportunity

In this section we want to outline the problem that exists and how this problem creates an opportunity for someone to solve it.

Here's the problem statement from the NeurTours plan:

> "In this day and age, business owners are under constant assault from technology: E-mail, fax, smartphones, landlines, social media, and 24/7 news. We're all connected around the clock, with little time to think. Further, entrepreneurs often feel like they're on an island, with no one who

> understands their issues. This creates an opportunity for anyone who can take them away from this bombardment of information to a place where they can unplug and collaborate with like-minded individuals."

I outlined the core problem my customers have in that that they're inundated with technology and constantly under assault and generally don't have a great support system of other like-minded entrepreneurs. It can be overwhelming. If you're an entrepreneur, you see NeurTours as an opportunity to unplug from all that and to get away, to refresh yourself and spend time with people who are going through some of the same things - all while experiencing some sort of bucket list adventure. That outlines the pain the customers are feeling and the opportunity the business addresses.

Executive Summary - The Solution

In this section, you'll explain how you're going to solve that customer pain, and how you're going to take advantage of that opportunity described in the previous section.

In the case of NeurTours, I describe how I gather small groups of successful entrepreneurs together for a challenging adventure while completely disconnecting them from technology, thus allowing them to focus on being creative, sharing ideas, developing plans. This freedom from the distractions of the office and everyday life, in addition to the stimulus of challenging adventure, beautiful scenery and the extremely powerful mastermind concept, will foster significant business breakthroughs.

Really, this section is a bit of a tease. You don't necessarily want to repeat your entire business model, but your do want to draw readers in and encourage them to read more. In my case, perhaps they want to learn more about the mastermind concept, or specific locations where we might be traveling. They need to read on to learn about that. This is another step along the path that we are trying to lead the audience.

Executive Summary - Success Factors

To this point, you've told people what the problem is, what the opportunity is and about your solution. What about your approach specifically is going to create success? Do you have some sort of competitive edge? What are your strengths as a as a team or as an individual? Is your location an advantage? Is your market underserved? Do you have a lot of experience in the industry?

Have you started companies before, and do you have a strong track record? Does your team?

Here is where you also want to mention that your product or service is in some way superior to anything else that is out there on the market. Will customer service be an advantage? Is your value proposition to customers better? Do you have a strong sales and marketing approach?

Executive Summary - Market Opportunity

This is the spot to outline the very highest level of your market research. If that section of the plan is the synthesis of all of the research you've done, then this section is a one- or two-line summary of that summary. Just the facts here, the high-level market size and how the market is trending. What is the future forecast for your market? If you hit those three points, you've covered a lot in a few words.

What you want to show here is that there is a market for what you're selling. You might also mention whether the market is consolidated with just a few large players or highly fragmented with dozens or even hundreds of competitors. Is there consolidation going on where some of the bigger players are buying up some of the smaller players, or are there a lot of new entrants flooding the market?

Executive Summary - Customers and Competition

Here you can briefly describe your avatar customer and perhaps mention a few of your biggest competitors. Again, you want to be very succinct.

For your avatar customer, what is their age, sex, income, their marital status, their hobbies, their likes and dislikes. Talk about how many of those potential customers exist. It shows that you've done your research, and it also shows that you maybe have some kind of customer validation where you know the types of people who are particularly interested.

If you've done a survey or other primary research mention it here.

For competitors, again, you want to pick out just the few of them, possibly names that the reader would be most likely to recognize. Discuss their market share and revenue volumes, if known. Again, just include high-level detail. You expand on this more in the competitor section.

Executive Summary - Other

There are a few other points of key data you want to include as you wrap up the all-important executive summary:

1) Management team - Just two or three key people here, not the whole team. And just a few of the most salient background points for each. You want the reader to want to learn more about your team.

2) Company information - When the company was formed, which state or country, what type of entity.

3) Your Contact Information - It should be on the cover, but restate it again here. You want to remind people that they can reach you directly and give them every opportunity to do so. Include a phone number, email, or any other pertinent contact info.

4) Financial - include a very condensed five-year financial forecast chart, and if you're raising capital, how much you need, and what it will be used for. Show how much you have personally invested in the company to date. Discuss exit strategies at a high level.

Executive Summary Long Term Vision

As a general rule, the time horizon of your business plan is going to be five years. You may, however, have some initiatives in mind that are longer term than that. You'll want to mention these, and state that they are not included in your current forecast, but they are in your plans for the future. Perhaps its new products or services that you expect to build at a later date. Or, it could be national or international expansion. Or perhaps you intend to turn your core business into a franchise.

Remember, as you wrap up your executive summary, that these few pages should be able to stand on their own as a separate document, but should also be a strong bridge to influence readers to fully dive into the complete business plan. If you've done a good job, your executive summary will do both.

11

GRAPHICS & EDITING

Graphics & Editing Introduction

Once everything is done with your plan, converting it to PDF is generally the way to go. It protects the integrity of your plan and makes it harder to change or screw up the formatting. If you decide to print your plan, PDF is usually the preferred format anyway. Places like Staples and Office Depot can print up really slick, colorful, spiral bound, covered copies for you that can leave a great impression. Don't cheap out with black and white unbound copies if you do print. After all, you've invested a lot of time and energy in your plan. Why not make it look its best?

If you're going to a meeting with an angel investor group, VCs, a family office, or just an individual, make sure you have enough copies for everyone who will be present. Never hurts to have a few extra copies on hand, either.

It should go without saying that you want to thoroughly edit your plan for typos and formatting issues. I like to read the plans I write for consulting clients out loud, as it generally helps me catch a lot of the errors or awkwardness that I might not catch in a read through. Make sure the fonts and indentations are all the same.

You also want to make sure that you break up the text with plenty of graphics and pictures. Not only does it help you convey your message with impact visuals, but it makes the reading experience more pleasant. A good plan should flow from one section to the next in a logical order. Your table of contents should be linked to the various sections such that you can click and jump to that section. Not everyone is going to read the plan in the order you intend, so making it easy to navigate is extremely helpful. There's nothing more annoying to a reader than having to hunt and search for specific information.

I had a client come to me from South Florida and he had spent quite a bit of money on his business plan, which another consultant created. He enlisted my help because he was getting a lot of negative feedback. When I read the plan created by this other consultant, honestly, the content was pretty good. On the flip side, it was so poorly formatted and organized, that it was just painful to read. It was difficult to find anything, and the writer actually had references to other sections throughout the plan that forced the reader to stop and then go out and search for the additional information. If you're reading, this kind of flipping back and forth is a nightmare. I was actually getting angry reading this plan, so I fully understood the negative feedback. It wasn't a terribly difficult chore to reorganize everything and make it cohesive, and once we did that, he started getting much more engagement, and ultimately, funding from his plan. It does make a difference.

Keep in mind, too, that some people are visual learners. Some people learn things by reading. Some people learn things by hearing. If you can provide people with different means of imparting that same information, that can be helpful.

Graphics & Charts
There are a lot of free or super inexpensive graphics you can include in your plan. Google images is a great source, but make sure you have permission to use the content. Some stock photo sites charge you to use their images, but there are plenty in the public domain that are free to use.

Of course, if you have pictures of your products, use those, particularly in your product/company section. If you're operating in a certain city, use pictures of the city. Use maps that you can print of where your business is located.

Another idea is to create your own graphics. If you've created a financial forecast, Excel has a lot of great graphics options. The base model we use at Blue Horizon Venture Consulting has some excellent graphics built into it (find out more at www.BrassTacksBooks.com/WWBP. There are some even cooler graphics packages out there where you can create amazing images. Spend some time on creating modern-looking graphics and they can add a ton of visual appeal to your plan.

Don't overdo it, however, just a few nice photos and charts that help you tell the story in your plan are all that is needed. It is possible to overload a plan with graphics that actually distract from the points you are trying to make versus enhance or reinforce them.

Proofreading & Editing
Read your plan many times. Spell check's going to catch a lot of your mistakes, but it's always good to read your plan aloud. Not only can you catch a lot of errors and odd wording, but this practice of speaking out loud about your

plan can also help you to prepare to speak to others about your business and can give you confidence. You may feel ridiculous doing it, but invariably it helps in multiple ways. You may even want to make an audio recording of you reading the plan. If you like it, you could actually send an MP3 recording to people who could perhaps listen to it while driving. You've saved them the work of reading it!

You also want to check for flow and make sure everything is presented logically. You may find some things that you want to change and correct.

12

CONCLUSION & SPECIAL OFFERS

OK, well this brings us to the end of our journey. It may be helpful to read this book once all the way through, and then read through it again as you are going through the first draft of your business plan.

You've done the research.

You built a financial model.

You put all the sections of the plan together.

You've written a very effective executive summary.

So now what?

Here at Blue Horizon Venture Consulting, we have a number of products and services that can help you on your journey.

For some of you, you may read this book and reach the conclusion that you just don't have the skill set, the time, and/or the desire to write your own plan. If not, we're happy to do all of the heavy lifting for you. Come on over to www.BlueHorizonVC.com, click on the Get Started button, and set up a free consultation call.

For others, you really want to give writing your own business plan a try, but you just need a helping hand to guide you along the way. We have a lower cost solution in the form of a guided course that gives you all of the templates, video instruction/demonstration, and live coaching calls where you can submit your questions and get answers. You can also opt for some additional one on one time with a professional consultant. To learn more about this guided course, please visit www.ToddHoustonSmith.com and join our next cohort!

And lastly, for the true do it yourselfer, we offer a number of tools and resources that can get you on your way. This book is an excellent guide to walk through the process. But we also have templates you can utilize, and other great resources. So please visit us at www.BrassTacksBooks.com/WWBP and see what we have to offer there.

And once you get your plan finished, we offer a service called the Business Plan Scorecard where you can get a detailed professional review of your business plan. We will read your entire plan, and evaluate each section on a variety of variables and present you with the comprehensive scorecard that lets you know at what level your business plan is "Investor Ready." Your goal is to get all green lights, at which point you are ready to start talking to investors.

Writing a winning business plan requires a lot of knowledge, effort, and dedication. But the results can be life altering. Instead of frustration, a good plan can lead to capitalization. Instead of a lack of strategic focus, a good plan can be like rocket fuel to your company's success.

But a plan is only a roadmap to these successes. Without execution, a plan will simply sit on a shelf gathering dust. It takes work to get in front of the right investors who have an interest in your stage, industry, and geography. Likewise, it takes work to execute on your strategic vision.

With grit, focus, and determination, and a world class business plan, you can get there.

To your success!!

9 781735 305936